Chevy II Nova

Power, Passion, and Performance

Todd Bandel

DEDICATION

I dedicate this book to all my past automotive mentors and colleagues. Your guidance, support, and shared wisdom have been invaluable in shaping my journey. Each of you played a significant role in my professional development, imparting knowledge and fostering a passion for excellence in the automotive field.

CONTENTS

ACKNOWLEDGEMENT   i

CHAPTER ONE

The Birth of an Icon: Introducing the Chevy II Nova   1

Chapter Two

From Compact to Muscle: The Evolution of the Nova's Design   17

Chapter Three

Under the Hood: Engineering Marvels of the Chevy II Nova   31

Chapter Four

The Nova in Pop Culture: A Symbol of American Automotive Prowess   49

Chapter Five

Chevrolet's Rising Star: How the Nova Shaped the Brand   65

Chapter Six

The Golden Age: Nova's Role in the Muscle Car Era   81

Chapter Seven

Innovations and Advancements: Nova's Technological Leaps   97

Chapter Eight

Behind the Wheel: Stories from Nova Owners and Drivers   113

Chapter Nine

Restoration Nation: The Art of Bringing Novas Back to Life   127

Chapter Ten

Nova vs. The World: Comparing the Chevy II to Its Rivals   141

Chapter Eleven

Collecting Nostalgia: The Nova in Today's Classic Car Market   155

Chapter Twelve

Legacy and Impact: The Chevy II Nova's Enduring Influence   173

ACKNOWLEDGMENTS

I want to express my deepest gratitude to my father for introducing me to the exhilarating world of automotive racing. Your passion for cars and dedication to the sport have inspired me.

From the first time you took me to a race track, I was captivated by the power and precision of the machines, as well as the skill required to master them.

Your guidance and support have fueled my interest and enthusiasm, making every moment in this thrilling world more meaningful. Thank you for sharing this incredible journey with me and for being such a pivotal influence in my life.

Chapter 1: The Birth of an Icon: Introducing the Chevy II Nova

Section 1.1: The Genesis of the Chevy II Nova

In the early 1960s, the automotive landscape was undergoing a significant transformation. American consumers, influenced by changing economic conditions and evolving preferences, began to show increased interest in compact cars. This shift presented both a challenge and an opportunity for major automakers, including Chevrolet.

Chevrolet, a division of General Motors, found itself in a precarious position. While the company had enjoyed tremendous success with its full-size models, it lacked a competitive offering in the rapidly growing compact car segment. The void in Chevrolet's lineup became glaringly apparent with the success of Ford's Falcon, which had been introduced in 1960 and quickly gained popularity among budget-conscious buyers.

Recognizing the urgent need to enter this market, Chevrolet's management set out to develop a new compact car that would appeal to a wide range of consumers. The goal was to create a vehicle that combined the practicality and efficiency of a compact with the style and performance that Chevrolet was known for.

The development process for what would become the Chevy II Nova was nothing short of remarkable. Under the leadership of chief engineer Ed Cole, the project went from concept to production in just 18 months - an impressive feat in automotive development, particularly for the time. This accelerated timeline was a testament to the importance Chevrolet placed on quickly entering the compact car market.

The naming of the new model was a crucial decision. Chevrolet wanted a name that would capture the essence of the car and resonate with potential buyers. After much deliberation, the name "Nova" was chosen. Derived from the Latin word for "new," Nova perfectly encapsulated the idea of a new star in the Chevrolet lineup. The full name "Chevy II Nova" combined the familiar Chevrolet brand with the promise of something new and exciting.

The initial design philosophy for the Chevy II Nova was centered on simplicity, functionality, and elegance. Designers aimed to create a car that would appeal to a wide range of consumers, from young families to retirees. The goal was to offer a compact car that didn't feel like a compromise, but rather a wise choice for the discerning buyer.

As the development process neared completion, excitement built within Chevrolet and its dealership network. The culmination of this anticipation came on September 29, 1961, when the first Chevy II Nova rolled off the production line in Willow Run, Michigan. This moment marked not just the birth of a new model but the beginning of a new era for Chevrolet.

The introduction of the Chevy II Nova was a pivotal moment for Chevrolet. It represented the company's ability to quickly adapt to changing market conditions and consumer preferences. More than just a new model, the Nova was Chevrolet's statement that it could compete and excel in every segment of the automotive market.

As the Chevy II Nova made its way to showrooms across the country, it was clear that Chevrolet had created something special. The car's combination of practicality, style, and value would soon make it a favorite among American car buyers, setting the stage for a legacy that would span decades.

Section 1.2: The First Generation Chevy II Nova (1962-1965)

The first generation of the Chevy II Nova, spanning from 1962 to 1965, marked the beginning of a legacy that would endure for decades. This inaugural iteration of the Nova showcased Chevrolet's commitment to versatility, affordability, and performance in the compact car segment.

Chevrolet offered the first-generation Chevy II in three distinct series, each catering to different consumer needs and preferences. The 100 Series served as the base model, providing an economical option for budget-conscious buyers. The 300 Series offered a step up in terms of features and comfort, while the Nova 400 Series represented the top-of-the-line option, boasting additional luxuries and performance capabilities. This tiered approach allowed Chevrolet to appeal to a wide range of customers, from those seeking a simple, reliable commuter car to those desiring a more upscale compact vehicle.

The body styles available for the first-generation Chevy II were equally diverse, reflecting the varied needs of American car buyers in the early 1960s. Customers could choose from a two-door coupe, a four-door sedan, a convertible, and even a station wagon. This variety of body styles ensured that the Chevy II could serve as everything from a stylish personal car to a practical family hauler.

Chevy II Nova: Power, Passion, and Performance

When it came to performance, the first-generation Chevy II initially offered two engine options. The base engine was a 153 cubic inch four-cylinder, which provided adequate power for everyday driving while emphasizing fuel efficiency. For those seeking more performance, a 194 cubic inch six-cylinder engine was available, offering a significant boost in power without sacrificing too much in terms of economy. In a move that would foreshadow the Nova's future as a performance icon, Chevrolet introduced a V8 option in 1964. This 283 cubic inch V8 engine transformed the Nova's performance capabilities, setting the stage for its eventual evolution into a muscle car.

The interior of the first-generation Chevy II Nova was designed with practicality and comfort in mind. The cabin featured clean, straightforward styling that prioritized functionality over flash. Bench seats were standard, providing ample room for passengers and reflecting the family-oriented nature of many compact car buyers. While the base models were relatively sparse in terms of amenities, higher trim levels and optional packages allowed buyers to customize their Novas with features like a push-button radio, upgraded upholstery, and additional interior trim.

Pricing played a crucial role in the Chevy II Nova's market positioning. With a starting price of $2,003 for the base model in 1962, the Chevy II was competitively priced against its main rivals, such as the Ford Falcon and Plymouth Valiant. This aggressive pricing strategy made the Nova an attractive option for budget-conscious buyers, young families, and those looking for an economical second car. As you moved up the trim levels and added options, the price naturally increased, but even fully-equipped models remained reasonably priced compared to larger, full-size cars.

The market reception for the first-generation Chevy II Nova was overwhelmingly positive. In its inaugural year, Chevrolet sold over 326,000 units, a clear indication that the Nova had struck a chord with American car buyers. This strong sales performance validated

Chevrolet's decision to enter the compact car market and demonstrated the Nova's appeal across a broad spectrum of consumers.

The success of the first-generation Chevy II Nova was not just about numbers, however. It quickly gained a reputation for reliability, practicality, and value, attributes that would become hallmarks of the Nova nameplate for years to come. Its combination of compact size, versatile body styles, and range of engine options allowed it to fill multiple roles in the market, from economical family car to budding performance machine.

As the first generation progressed, Chevrolet continued to refine and improve the Nova, responding to customer feedback and market trends. These ongoing enhancements, coupled with its strong initial reception, laid a solid foundation for the Nova's future success and established it as a key player in Chevrolet's lineup. The first-generation Chevy II Nova not only met the immediate needs of compact car buyers in the early 1960s but also set the stage for the model's evolution into an automotive icon.

Section 1.3: The Nova's Place in Chevrolet's Lineup

The introduction of the Chevy II Nova in 1962 marked a significant moment for Chevrolet, as it filled a crucial gap in their product lineup. This new compact model was strategically positioned to compete in a growing market segment while complementing Chevrolet's existing offerings.

Within Chevrolet's diverse range of vehicles, the Nova found its niche between the smaller, rear-engined Corvair and the larger, full-size Chevrolet models. This positioning allowed Chevrolet to offer a more conventional compact car option to consumers who were hesitant about the Corvair's unique rear-engine design. The Nova's front-engine, rear-wheel-drive layout provided a familiar driving experience that appealed to a broad audience.

Chevy II Nova: Power, Passion, and Performance

Chevrolet aimed the Nova at a specific demographic: young families, first-time car buyers, and those seeking an economical second car. Its compact size made it ideal for urban environments, while its practicality and affordability appealed to budget-conscious consumers. The Nova's versatility allowed it to serve multiple purposes, from a reliable daily driver to a weekend family car.

The marketing strategies employed to promote the Nova emphasized its practicality, affordability, and American-made quality. Chevrolet's advertising campaigns highlighted the car's efficiency, ease of maintenance, and value for money. Slogans such as "Chevy II - The Great In-Between Size" highlighted its position in the lineup and its ability to cater to diverse consumer needs.

Chevrolet dealers received the Nova with enthusiasm, seeing it as a versatile addition to their showrooms that could attract a wide range of customers. The Nova's presence in dealerships allowed salespeople to offer a compact option to customers who found full-size models too large or expensive, potentially capturing sales that might otherwise have gone to competitors.

The introduction of the Nova had a significant impact on Chevrolet's overall brand image. It reinforced Chevrolet's reputation as a brand that offered something for everyone, from economy cars to luxury models. The Nova demonstrated Chevrolet's ability to respond quickly to market trends and consumer demands, enhancing the brand's image as innovative and customer-focused.

Moreover, the Nova's success in the compact car segment helped Chevrolet maintain its competitive edge against rivals like Ford and Plymouth. It showed that Chevrolet could produce a successful conventional compact car, countering any perception that the brand was overly reliant on the unconventional Corvair in this market segment.

As the Nova established itself in Chevrolet's lineup, it began to develop its own identity within the brand. While initially focused on economy and practicality, the model would later evolve to include performance variants, foreshadowing its future role in Chevrolet's muscle car lineup.

The Nova's position in Chevrolet's range also allowed for interesting cross-pollination of features and technologies. Innovations tested on the Nova could be scaled up for larger models. At the same time, some features from higher-end Chevrolets could be adapted for use in the compact Nova, providing value to customers across different price points.

In essence, the introduction of the Chevy II Nova not only filled a gap in Chevrolet's product range but also played a crucial role in shaping the brand's identity and market strategy in the 1960s. Its success demonstrated Chevrolet's adaptability and reinforced the brand's position as a leader in the American automotive industry, capable of meeting diverse consumer needs with a single, well-conceived model.

Section 1.4: Early Innovations and Unique Features

The Chevy II Nova wasn't just another compact car in Chevrolet's lineup; it was a vehicle that brought several innovations and unique features to the market. From its advanced chassis design to its focus on fuel efficiency, the Nova showcased Chevrolet's commitment to pushing the boundaries of automotive engineering.

One of the most notable features of the Nova was its chassis and suspension design. The car utilized a unibody construction, which was relatively advanced for its time. This design approach integrated the body and frame into a single unit, offering improved rigidity and significant weight savings compared to traditional body-on-frame constructions. The result was a car that felt more solid on the road and offered better handling characteristics than many of its competitors. The unibody design also allowed for more interior space, making the Nova feel roomier than its compact exterior dimensions might suggest.

Fuel efficiency was another area where the Nova shone. In an era when gas-guzzling V8s were becoming increasingly popular, the Nova offered a range of efficient engine options. The base 153 cubic-inch four-cylinder engine and the 194 cubic-inch six-cylinder engine were both designed with fuel economy in mind. These efficient powerplants, combined with the Nova's lightweight design, made it one of the more fuel-efficient options in Chevrolet's lineup. This focus on efficiency resonated with budget-conscious buyers and those looking for a practical daily driver.

Safety was also a key consideration in the Nova's design. While safety features were not as comprehensive as they are in modern vehicles, the Nova did introduce some noteworthy advancements. In 1964, Chevrolet made front seat belts standard equipment on the Nova, ahead of many competitors and before it became a federal requirement. This move demonstrated Chevrolet's commitment to passenger safety and helped position the Nova as a responsible choice for families.

Customization was another area where the Nova excelled. Chevrolet offered a wide range of paint colors, interior options, and performance upgrades, allowing buyers to personalize their Novas to suit their tastes and needs. This versatility was a significant selling point, appealing to a broad spectrum of customers, from practical family car buyers to young enthusiasts seeking a car they could modify and make their own.

Technologically, the Nova incorporated several features that were considered advanced for its time. The optional Powerglide automatic transmission was a significant technological feature, offering smooth and efficient gear changes. This two-speed automatic transmission was well-suited to the Nova's compact car character, providing a balance of performance and efficiency. For those who preferred more control, a three-speed manual transmission was also available.

The Nova's instrument panel was another area of innovation. It featured a clean, modern design with easy-to-read gauges and controls placed within easy reach of the driver. This focus on ergonomics and usability was ahead of its time and contributed to the Nova's reputation as a driver-friendly car.

In terms of comfort features, the Nova offered several options that were impressive for a compact car of its era. These included an optional push-button radio, heater, and defroster, and even air conditioning in later models. These features allowed the Nova to compete with larger, more expensive cars in terms of comfort and convenience.

The Nova's early innovations and unique features set it apart from the competition and laid the groundwork for its future success. By combining practical engineering with thoughtful design and a focus on user needs, Chevrolet created a car that was more than just transportation – it was a versatile, efficient, and enjoyable companion for a wide range of drivers. These qualities would continue to define the Nova throughout its production run, cementing its place in automotive history.

Section 1.5: Early Motorsports and Performance Achievements

The Chevy II Nova quickly made its mark in the world of motorsports, particularly in drag racing. Almost immediately after its introduction, enthusiasts recognized the Nova's potential as a lightweight, robust platform for racing. Its compact size and relatively low weight made it an ideal candidate for modification and high-performance applications.

Chevy II Nova: Power, Passion, and Performance

Drag racing became the Nova's first arena of competitive success. The car's combination of a short wheelbase, light weight, and the ability to accommodate larger engines made it a favorite among racers looking for a winning edge. As early as 1963, modified Novas began appearing at drag strips across the country, often outperforming more established muscle cars.

One of the most notable figures in early Nova racing was Bill "Grumpy" Jenkins, a legendary drag racer and engine builder. Jenkins achieved remarkable success with modified Chevy II Novas in the mid-1960s, helping to cement the car's reputation as a serious performance contender. His victories in National Hot Rod Association (NHRA) events brought widespread attention to the Nova's potential and inspired countless other racers to adopt the platform.

Recognizing the growing enthusiasm for performance, Chevrolet introduced the Super Sport (SS) package for the Nova in 1964. This marked the Nova's official entry into the performance car market and provided a factory-backed option for those seeking more power and sportier handling. The SS package typically included visual enhancements, such as special badging and trim, along with performance upgrades, including a more powerful engine and improved suspension components.

The success of performance-oriented Novas had a significant impact on future Chevrolet models. The lessons learned from racing and high-performance street applications of the Nova influenced the development of later muscle cars in the Chevrolet lineup. The Nova's success demonstrated the market's appetite for compact, powerful vehicles and helped pave the way for iconic models like the Camaro.

Early Novas set several notable performance records, further enhancing the model's reputation. At the 1964 NHRA Winternationals, a modified Nova set a class record, showcasing the model's performance potential to a national audience. This achievement, along with numerous local and regional racing successes, helped establish the Nova as a force to be reckoned with in motorsports circles.

The Nova's early racing success wasn't limited to the drag strip. Some enthusiasts also modified Novas for road racing and stock car events, demonstrating the car's versatility as a performance platform. While not as common as its drag racing applications, these efforts further broadened the Nova's appeal among automotive enthusiasts.

As the 1960s progressed, the Nova became increasingly popular as a basis for home-built hot rods and custom cars. Its simple design and readily available aftermarket parts made it an ideal choice for enthusiasts looking to create unique, high-performance vehicles. This grassroots enthusiasm further fueled the Nova's reputation as a performance car and contributed to its enduring popularity.

The early motorsports and performance achievements of the Chevy II Nova played a crucial role in shaping the car's identity. What began as a practical, economical compact quickly evolved into a respected performer, setting the stage for the Nova's future as a true muscle car icon. These early successes not only boosted sales and enthusiasm for the Nova but also helped establish Chevrolet as a major player in the growing performance car market of the 1960s.

Section 1.6: Critical Reception and Reviews

The introduction of the Chevy II Nova in 1962 generated significant buzz in the automotive world, drawing attention from industry experts, journalists, and consumers alike. The automotive press quickly took notice of this new compact offering from Chevrolet, with many publications eager to put the Nova through its paces and share their thoughts with readers.

Car and Driver, one of the most respected automotive publications of the time, praised the Nova's practicality and value, calling it "a sensible American compact with a dash of style." This sentiment was echoed by many other reviewers who appreciated the Nova's blend of functionality and aesthetic appeal. The car's clean lines and no-nonsense design were seen as a refreshing departure from some of the more ostentatious offerings of the era.

When compared to its main competitors, the Nova often came out on top in key areas. In comparison tests, it frequently outperformed the Ford Falcon in handling and interior space. Reviewers noted that while the Falcon may have been the first American compact to market, the Nova felt more refined and better executed. The Nova's superior handling was attributed to its well-designed suspension system, which provided a comfortable ride without sacrificing responsiveness.

The Nova's range of engine options also received positive attention. While the base four-cylinder engine was praised for its efficiency, it was the optional six-cylinder and later V8 engines that really caught the eye of performance-minded reviewers. These more powerful options were seen as giving the Nova a versatility that many of its competitors lacked, allowing it to appeal to a broader range of buyers.

The Nova's success was not just limited to positive reviews; it also garnered several prestigious awards. In a testament to its overall excellence, the 1963 Chevy II Nova was named "Car of the Year" by Motor Trend magazine. This accolade cemented the Nova's status as a standout in its class and helped to boost its popularity among consumers.

Consumer Reports, known for its unbiased and thorough testing, also weighed in on the Nova. They noted the car's reliability and fuel efficiency, recommending it as a wise choice for budget-conscious buyers. This endorsement from such a trusted source likely played a significant role in Nova's success in the marketplace.

Chevy II Nova: Power, Passion, and Performance

Early consumer feedback on the Nova was generally positive. Many buyers appreciated the car's affordability, practicality, and ease of maintenance. The Nova quickly gained a reputation as a dependable, no-nonsense vehicle that could handle the daily commute as well as weekend family trips. Some owners did note that the base model could feel underpowered, but this criticism was often offset by praise for the car's fuel economy.

The Nova's introduction had a significant impact on the compact car segment as a whole. Its success prompted other manufacturers to reassess their compact car offerings, leading to increased competition and innovation in the segment. This ripple effect ultimately benefited consumers, as automakers strove to match or exceed the Nova's combination of style, practicality, and value.

Interestingly, the Nova's influence extended beyond the compact car category. Its success demonstrated to Chevrolet and other manufacturers that there was a market for smaller cars that could still offer performance options. This realization would later play a role in the development of the muscle car era, with the Nova itself evolving to become a platform for high-performance variants.

Critics also praised the Nova's interior design and comfort features. While not luxurious, the cabin was described as well-thought-out and ergonomic. The simplicity of the dashboard layout was appreciated, as was the ample headroom and legroom, especially considering the car's compact exterior dimensions.

However, the Nova wasn't without its critics. Some reviewers felt that its styling, while clean and functional, was perhaps too conservative. Some believed that Chevrolet had played it too safe with the Nova, suggesting that a more daring design could have made an even bigger splash in the market.

Despite these minor criticisms, the overall critical reception of the Chevy II Nova was overwhelmingly positive. It was seen as a well-executed entry into the compact car market, offering a compelling blend of practicality, affordability, and subtle style. The numerous positive reviews, comparison test victories, and prestigious awards all contributed to the Nova's strong sales and enduring popularity.

The Nova's warm reception by critics and consumers alike set the stage for its future success and evolution. It had proven that Chevrolet could compete effectively in the compact car segment, establishing a solid foundation upon which future generations of the model could build. The positive critical reception of the Nova in its early years would play a crucial role in cementing its place in automotive history and in the hearts of car enthusiasts for decades to come.

Section 1.7: The Nova's Early Cultural Impact

The Chevy II Nova's influence extended far beyond the automotive world, quickly embedding itself into the fabric of 1960s American culture. From the silver screen to suburban driveways, the Nova's presence was felt across various facets of society.

In the realm of media, the Nova made several notable appearances that helped cement its place in the public consciousness. One of the most memorable was its role in the star-studded 1963 comedy film "It's a Mad, Mad, Mad, Mad World." This cameo introduced the Nova to a broad audience, showcasing its sleek design and practicality to moviegoers nationwide. The car's appearances in popular TV shows and advertisements further solidified its status as a cultural icon of the era.

As the Nova's popularity grew, so did the enthusiasm of its owners. By 1964, the first Chevy II Nova owners club was formed in California. This marked the beginning of a passionate and enduring enthusiast community. These clubs provided a platform for Nova owners to share their experiences, exchange maintenance tips, and showcase their customized vehicles. The formation of these communities highlighted the Nova's ability to inspire loyalty and camaraderie among its owners, a trait that would continue throughout its production run.

The Nova struck a particular chord with young car buyers and enthusiasts. Its affordability and customizable nature made it an attractive option for first-time car owners. Many young drivers saw the Nova as more than just a means of transportation; it was a canvas for personal expression. The ease with which the Nova could be modified, coupled with its potential for performance upgrades, made it a favorite among the youth culture of the 1960s. From custom paint jobs to engine swaps, the Nova became a reflection of its owner's personality and aspirations.

The Nova's popularity wasn't uniform across the country, however. It found particular success in urban areas, where its compact size and efficiency were highly valued. City dwellers appreciated the Nova's ability to navigate crowded streets and fit into tight parking spaces, all while providing the comfort and style of a larger car. In suburban areas, the Nova often served as a practical second car for families, further expanding its reach across different demographics.

As the 1960s progressed, the Nova began to symbolize certain aspects of the era itself. It embodied the practical yet aspirational spirit of early 1960s America. On one hand, it represented sensibility and efficiency, aligning with the pragmatic values of the time. On the other hand, its potential for customization and performance hinted at the individualism and power that would come to define the latter part of the decade. The Nova straddled the line between the conservative 1950s and the more expressive late 1960s, making it an accurate automotive representation of a changing America.

The Nova's cultural impact during these early years laid the foundation for its enduring legacy. It wasn't just a car; it was a symbol of accessibility, potential, and American ingenuity. As we'll see in the following chapters, this cultural resonance would only grow stronger as the Nova evolved, solidifying its place not just in automotive history, but also in American cultural history.

Chapter 2: From Compact to Muscle: The Evolution of the Nova's Design

Section 2.1: The Birth of the Chevy II (1962-1965)

The Chevy II made its debut in 1962, marking Chevrolet's entry into the burgeoning compact car market. Conceived as a response to the success of Ford's Falcon and other compact competitors, the Chevy II was designed with simplicity and economy in mind. Unlike its more complex cousin, the rear-engined Corvair, the Chevy II featured a conventional front-engine, rear-wheel-drive layout that appealed to conservative American car buyers.

The initial design philosophy behind the Chevy II was rooted in practicality and affordability. Chevrolet's goal was to create a no-frills, reliable vehicle that could compete directly with the Ford Falcon in terms of price and features. This approach resulted in a car that was noticeably more austere than the Corvair, but one that resonated with budget-conscious consumers looking for straightforward transportation.

Chevy II Nova: Power, Passion, and Performance

The first-generation Chevy II boasted clean, understated styling that set it apart from its more flamboyant full-size counterparts. A boxy silhouette with crisp lines and minimal ornamentation characterized its design. The front end featured a simple grille with horizontal bars, flanked by round headlights. Chrome accents were used sparingly, adding a touch of brightness to the otherwise modest exterior.

One of the Chevy II's key strengths was its variety of body styles. Chevrolet offered the compact in several configurations, including a two-door coupe, four-door sedan, and station wagon. This versatility allowed the Chevy II to appeal to a wide range of customers, from small families to young professionals.

In 1963, Chevrolet introduced the Nova as a premium trim level for the Chevy II. The Nova package elevated the car's appeal with additional features and more refined styling cues. Nova models received extra chrome trim, upgraded interior materials, and more comprehensive standard equipment. This move not only broadened the Chevy II's market appeal but also laid the groundwork for the Nova to become the primary nameplate for the model eventually.

The mid-cycle refresh of 1964-1965 brought subtle but significant changes to the Chevy II's design. The front end received a facelift, featuring a wider grille with a more pronounced horizontal emphasis. The headlights were now set in chrome bezels, adding a touch of sophistication to the car's appearance. Interior refinements included a redesigned instrument panel and improved seating comfort, addressing some of the criticisms of the earlier models' basic cabin.

Public reception of the first-generation Chevy II Nova was generally positive. Consumers appreciated its straightforward design, reliable mechanics, and affordable price point. While it may not have garnered the same enthusiasm as some of Chevrolet's sportier offerings, the Chevy II found a loyal following among practical-minded buyers.

Sales figures for the Chevy II were respectable, though they never quite matched those of the Ford Falcon. In its first year, Chevrolet sold over 326,000 Chevy IIs, a solid performance for a new model. However, the Falcon had a head start in the market and maintained its sales lead throughout most of the first generation. Despite this, the Chevy II managed to carve out a significant niche in the compact car segment, establishing itself as a worthy competitor and laying the foundation for future success.

As the first generation drew to a close, it was clear that the Chevy II had made its mark. Its evolution from a bare-bones compact to offering the more upscale Nova trim demonstrated Chevrolet's responsiveness to market demands. The stage was set for a more dramatic transformation in the coming years, as the automotive landscape began to shift towards performance, and the Nova would soon find itself at the forefront of the muscle car era.

Section 2.2: The Second Generation (1966-1967)

The Chevy II Nova underwent a significant transformation in 1966, ushering in its second generation with a bold new design that signaled a shift towards a more performance-oriented image. Gone was the boxy, utilitarian look of the first generation, replaced by a sleeker, more muscular profile that turned heads and hinted at the power lurking beneath the hood.

The redesigned Nova boasted a longer, lower stance with flowing lines that gave it a sense of motion even when parked. The front end featured a more aggressive grille, flanked by dual headlights that provided a menacing stare. The rear quarter panels gained subtle curves, creating a more cohesive and sporty appearance. This new look was a stark departure from its predecessor, as evident when comparing side-by-side images of the 1965 and 1966 models. The transformation was nothing short of remarkable, with the '66 Nova looking like a completely different car.

Chevy II Nova: Power, Passion, and Performance

Chevrolet's shift towards a sportier image for the Nova was not just skin deep. The introduction of the Super Sport (SS) package in 1966 further cemented the car's new performance aspirations. The SS trim added distinctive badging, special wheel covers, and a sportier interior, visually setting it apart from the standard Nova. This move was a clear indication that Chevrolet was positioning the Nova to compete in the burgeoning muscle car market.

The expanded engine options available for the second-generation Nova had a profound impact on its design and identity. The availability of larger, more powerful V8 engines necessitated changes to the car's structure and appearance. Most notably, V8-equipped Novas featured a subtle but distinctive power bulge on the hood, hinting at the potent powerplant beneath. This visual cue became a hallmark of performance-oriented Novas and added to the car's muscular aesthetic.

Inside, the Nova's interior received significant upgrades to match its more upscale exterior. The dashboard was redesigned with a more modern look, featuring a horizontal speedometer and cleaner lines. The seats were restyled for improved comfort and support, with the SS models receiving special trim and upholstery. The overall effect was a more driver-focused cockpit that complemented the car's sportier character.

The design changes implemented in the second-generation Nova had a significant impact on its market positioning. No longer just an economical compact, the Nova now appealed to a broader range of customers, including performance enthusiasts. Period advertisements reflect this shift, with copy highlighting the Nova's "bold new look" and "sports car feel." One ad proclaimed, "Nova SS: The Chevrolet that's something else," emphasizing its departure from the previous generation's modest image.

Despite its short two-year run, the second-generation Nova played a crucial role in the model's evolution. It bridged the gap between the utilitarian first generation and the full-fledged muscle car that would emerge in 1968. The design changes introduced in 1966-1967 set the stage for the Nova's most iconic years, establishing it as a serious contender in the performance car market. This brief but impactful generation demonstrated Chevrolet's ability to adapt quickly to changing consumer preferences, transforming the Nova from a practical compact into a stylish, desirable performance machine.

Section 2.3: The Third Generation (1968-1974)

The year 1968 marked a pivotal moment in the Nova's history with the introduction of the third generation. This redesign represented a dramatic departure from its predecessors, fully embracing the muscle car aesthetic that had taken hold of the American automotive landscape. The new Nova boasted a longer wheelbase and a more aggressive stance, signaling its evolution from a modest compact to a formidable contender in the performance car segment.

The most striking feature of the 1968 Nova was its fastback-inspired roofline, which gave the car a sleek, aerodynamic profile. This design element not only enhanced the car's visual appeal but also improved its performance characteristics. The front end featured a bold, wide grille that extended across the entire width of the car, flanked by dual headlights that added to its menacing appearance. The sculptured body lines running along the sides created a sense of motion even when the vehicle was stationary, emphasizing its performance potential.

As the muscle car era reached its zenith, the Nova's design fully incorporated performance-oriented styling cues. The hood bulged subtly to accommodate larger engines, while the wheel arches were slightly flared to house wider tires. These design elements not only served functional purposes but also conveyed a sense of power and speed that resonated with enthusiasts.

However, the Nova's evolution during this period wasn't solely driven by performance considerations. The late 1960s and early 1970s saw the introduction of new safety regulations that had a significant impact on automotive design. The Nova adapted to these requirements while maintaining its muscular aesthetic. For instance, the bumpers were redesigned to meet new impact standards, becoming more prominent features of the car's overall design. Lighting elements were also updated, with larger taillights and side marker lights being integrated more seamlessly into the body lines.

The Super Sport (SS) package, which had been introduced in the previous generation, reached new heights of popularity during this period. The SS trim level featured distinctive badging, often including bold stripes along the sides or over the trunk lid. Special SS wheels and unique color options further set these performance models apart from their standard counterparts.

Throughout the third generation's lifespan, from 1968 to 1974, the Nova underwent several updates and refreshes to keep it current with changing tastes and regulations. One of the most notable changes came in 1973 when the front end was redesigned. This update featured a more pronounced grille and a revised bumper design to meet new five-mile-per-hour impact standards. Despite these changes, the overall muscular character of the third-generation Nova remained intact.

The interior of the third-generation Nova also reflected its more premium positioning. The dashboard was redesigned with a focus on driver-oriented controls, often featuring round gauges housed in deep, chrome-rimmed pods. Higher-end models offered wood-grain accents and more luxurious upholstery options, bridging the gap between performance and comfort.

By the end of the third generation in 1974, the Nova had completed its transformation from an economy compact to an actual muscle car. Its design language spoke volumes about the changing automotive landscape of the late 1960s and early 1970s, capturing the spirit of an era defined by performance, style, and the emerging influence of safety regulations. The third-generation Nova remains one of the most iconic iterations of the model, cherished by enthusiasts for its perfect blend of aggressive styling and classic muscle car proportions.

Section 2.4: The Fourth and Final Generation (1975-1979)

As the mid-1970s approached, the automotive landscape was shifting dramatically. The Nova, once a symbol of compact simplicity, turned muscle car contender, was about to undergo its final transformation. The fourth-generation Nova, introduced in 1975, represented a significant departure from its predecessors, adopting a more squared-off, formal styling that reflected the evolving tastes of American consumers.

Gone were the swooping lines and aggressive stance of the third-generation models. In their place stood a boxier, more upright design that prioritized practicality and comfort over performance aesthetics. The front end featured a larger, more prominent grille, flanked by rectangular headlights that gave the car a wider, more planted appearance. The hood, once adorned with power bulges, now lay flat and unassuming, hinting at the shifting focus away from raw horsepower.

This design shift wasn't merely a stylistic choice; it was a response to the evolving market preferences of the time. As fuel prices rose and economic uncertainties loomed, car buyers began to favor vehicles that projected an image of sensibility and efficiency. The Nova's new look, with its clean lines and less ostentatious presence, appealed to those seeking a more mature, restrained automobile.

However, the Nova's transformation wasn't solely driven by market forces. Stricter emissions and safety standards played a significant role in shaping the car's new identity. The most noticeable change came in the form of larger, more robust bumpers designed to meet new impact regulations. These substantial bumpers, particularly prominent on the 1975 and 1976 models, gave the Nova a somewhat bulky appearance, especially when compared to the sleek designs of earlier years.

Despite the move towards a more conservative image, Chevrolet didn't entirely abandon the Nova's performance heritage. The Super Sport (SS) package continued to be offered, paying homage to the car's muscle car heritage. However, the SS trim of this era was a far cry from its tire-shredding predecessors. The distinctive SS graphics and trim of the late '70s models were more about visual flair than performance promise, featuring bold striping and unique wheel designs that added a sporty touch to the otherwise subdued styling.

As the Nova approached the end of its production run, its design reflected nearly two decades of evolution. The final iterations of the Nova in 1978 and 1979 saw subtle refinements, with a slightly more aerodynamic front end and improved integration of the federally mandated safety features. These last models represented a car that had matured alongside its original customer base, offering a blend of the practical sensibility that defined its early years with a touch of the performance spirit it embraced in its prime.

Comparing the 1979 Nova to its 1962 ancestor reveals a striking visual journey. While the two cars shared little in terms of design language, they both embodied the spirit of their respective eras. The original Chevy II Nova was a testament to the optimism and simplicity of the early '60s. At the same time, the final fourth-generation Nova reflected the pragmatism and changing priorities of the late '70s.

As production of the Nova came to an end in 1979, it left behind a design legacy that spanned from the height of the muscle car era to the dawn of the efficiency-focused '80s. The fourth and final generation may not have been the most beloved in terms of styling.

Still, it represented a crucial chapter in Nova's story, one of adaptation and survival in a rapidly changing automotive landscape.

Section 2.5: Design Influence and Legacy

The Chevrolet Nova's design journey from 1962 to 1979 left an indelible mark on automotive history, influencing not only other Chevrolet models but also shaping the broader landscape of American car design. Throughout its production run, the Nova's evolving aesthetics reflected changing consumer tastes, technological advancements, and shifting market demands, making it a fascinating case study in automotive design evolution.

The Nova's influence on other Chevrolet models was significant and far-reaching. Design elements pioneered or popularized by the Nova often found their way into other vehicles in the Chevrolet lineup. For instance, the aggressive front-end styling of the third-generation Nova, with its bold grille and quad headlights, inspired similar treatments in models like the Chevelle and Camaro. The Nova's clean, muscular lines and purposeful stance became a template for Chevrolet's performance-oriented vehicles, helping to establish a cohesive design language across the brand's offerings.

In the broader context of automotive design history, the Nova holds a unique position. Its evolution from a compact, economical car to a muscular performance vehicle, and then back to a more comfort-oriented sedan, mirrors the changing priorities of American car buyers over nearly two decades. The Nova's design progression serves as a visual timeline of automotive trends, from the chrome-laden aesthetics of the early 1960s to the more austere, fuel-efficiency-focused designs of the late 1970s.

Among enthusiasts, certain generations and design elements of the Nova continue to hold particular appeal. The clean, classic lines of the first-generation models are prized for their simplicity and purity of form. However, it's the third-generation Nova, particularly the 1968-

1972 models, that often commands the most attention at classic car shows and auctions. These models, with their perfect blend of muscular proportions and sleek detailing, represent the Nova at its peak of performance and aesthetic appeal. Data from recent Barrett-Jackson auctions shows that well-preserved or restored third-generation Novas, especially those with SS trim, consistently fetch premium prices, underscoring their enduring popularity.

The Nova's design legacy extended beyond its production years, influencing future Chevrolet compact cars. While subsequent models like the Cavalier and Cobalt were developed in response to different market conditions, traces of the Nova's DNA can be seen in their designs. The emphasis on clean lines, a strong horizontal grille element, and a slight wedge profile - all hallmarks of later Nova designs - found expression in these successor models, albeit adapted for more modern sensibilities.

In today's automotive landscape, where retro-inspired designs have gained popularity, the Nova's influence can still be felt. The current generation Chevrolet Camaro, for instance, incorporates design cues reminiscent of classic muscle cars, including some that echo the Nova's most iconic years. The Camaro's strong shoulder line, aggressive stance, and the way the greenhouse tapers towards the rear are all elements that can be traced back to the muscle car era that the Nova helped define.

The Nova's design evolution from 1962 to 1979 is more than just a story of one car's changing appearance. It reflects American culture, technological progress, and shifting automotive priorities. From its humble beginnings as a simple compact to its muscular mid-life crisis and its final years as a comfortable cruiser, the Nova's design journey encapsulates nearly two decades of automotive history. Its influence continues to resonate in the world of car design, serving as a touchstone for enthusiasts and a source of inspiration for modern designers looking to capture the essence of classic American automobiles.

Section 2.6: The Nova's Design Impact on Pop Culture

The Chevrolet Nova's evolving design didn't just impact the automotive world; it left an indelible mark on American pop culture. As the car transformed from a modest compact to a muscular icon, it became a symbol of changing times and shifting attitudes in America.

In the early 1960s, the clean, simple lines of the first-generation Chevy II Nova reflected the optimism and straightforward values of the era. It was the kind of car you'd see parked in driveways on TV shows like "Leave It to Beaver" or "The Andy Griffith Show," representing the attainable American dream for middle-class families.

As the Nova embraced a sportier image in the mid-1960s, it began appearing in youth-oriented movies and TV shows. The 1966 model, with its more aggressive styling, became a favorite of young characters in coming-of-age stories, symbolizing freedom and rebellion. It wasn't uncommon to see a Nova screeching its tires in hot pursuit scenes on popular cop shows of the late '60s and early '70s.

The third-generation Nova, with its full embrace of muscle car aesthetics, became a staple in Hollywood productions. Its aggressive stance and powerful presence made it a natural choice for action movies and TV series. The Nova's appearance cemented its status as an icon of 1960s youth culture, despite the film being set a decade earlier. This anachronistic use speaks volumes about how deeply the Nova had become associated with a particular era and attitude in the American consciousness.

In the music world, the Nova found its way into countless song lyrics, particularly in the rock and country genres. Artists used the Nova as shorthand for a particular kind of American experience, sometimes representing freedom and adventure, other times standing in for lost youth or simpler times.

Chevy II Nova: Power, Passion, and Performance

The fourth-generation Nova's more subdued styling coincided with a shift in pop culture representations. As the muscle car era faded, the Nova began to appear more frequently as a reliable, if somewhat mundane, mode of transportation in TV shows and movies set in the late '70s and early '80s. This shift mirrored the changing priorities of American car buyers, from performance to practicality.

Even after its production ended, the Nova continued to make appearances in period pieces and nostalgic works. Its various iterations served as visual shorthand for specific eras, helping to establish the time period of a scene or story instantly.

In recent years, the resurgence of interest in classic cars has brought the Nova back into the spotlight. Restored Novas, particularly the performance-oriented models, have become sought-after props in films and TV shows seeking to evoke a sense of '60s and '70s Americana. The Nova's appearance in modern media often serves as a touchstone for authenticity in period representations.

Beyond the screen, the Nova's design has inspired artists, becoming a subject for paintings, sculptures, and even elaborate custom car builds that pay homage to its iconic lines. Car enthusiasts and artists alike have been drawn to the Nova's evolution, seeing in its changing design a reflection of America's own journey through the turbulent decades of the '60s and '70s.

The Nova's enduring presence in pop culture speaks to the power of its design. From its humble beginnings to its muscular heyday and comfortable final form, the Nova's visual language has become an integral part of how we visually represent and remember mid-20th-century America. Its journey from practical family car to performance icon to nostalgic symbol mirrors the complex and ever-changing American cultural landscape, ensuring its place not only in automotive history but also in the broader tapestry of American pop culture.

Section 2.7: The Compact Car Revolution

Under the leadership of Clare MacKichan, Chevrolet's design team approached the Chevy II with a clear mission: create an economical vehicle that would appeal to budget-conscious consumers while maintaining the quality and reliability that customers expected from the Chevrolet brand. The resulting design emphasized function over extravagance, featuring clean lines and an uncluttered aesthetic that reflected its down-to-earth purpose.

Unlike the Ford Falcon with its rounded, European-influenced styling, the Chevy II embraced a distinctly American design language characterized by squared-off proportions and straightforward visual elements. This no-nonsense approach pervaded every aspect of the car, from its boxy silhouette to the simple, horizontal grille that defined its face. The 1962 Chevy II's front end featured this understated grille flanked by round headlights, with chrome accents applied judiciously to add refinement without compromising the car's modest character.

Chevrolet offered the first-generation Chevy II in an impressive array of body styles, ensuring there was a variant for virtually every need. Consumers could select from two-door coupes, four-door sedans, convertibles, and practical station wagons, each maintaining the vehicle's core design philosophy while offering features tailored to different lifestyles.

In 1963, a significant development occurred when Chevrolet introduced the Nova as a premium trim level for the Chevy II. This strategic move positioned the model to compete more effectively against higher-end compact offerings in the market. The Nova package enhanced the car's appeal through additional exterior trim, upgraded interior materials, and more sophisticated instrumentation, elevating the vehicle's status while preserving its fundamental design principles.

Chevy II Nova: Power, Passion, and Performance

The Nova trim package proved immediately popular with consumers, gradually becoming so closely associated with the Chevy II that the two names became nearly inseparable in the public consciousness. It offered drivers the opportunity to enjoy compact car practicality without sacrificing status or comfort, a combination that resonated strongly with buyers. This success foreshadowed the vehicle's eventual evolution toward performance-oriented variants in later years.

The model received a thoughtful mid-cycle refresh for the 1964 and 1965 model years. These updates, although subtle, played a crucial role in refining the car's appearance and maintaining its competitiveness in the rapidly evolving compact market. Designers paid particular attention to the front end, implementing a revised grille design and more pronounced headlight bezels. Inside, passengers benefited from improvements to both styling and comfort, including redesigned seats and updated trim options.

Throughout its first generation, the Chevy II Nova enjoyed a strong reception from consumers and automotive critics alike. It's honest, unpretentious design philosophy connected with buyers seeking reliability and affordability without compromise on quality. Sales performance remained robust, with the Chevy II Nova frequently outpacing its domestic competition.

By the time the first generation concluded in 1965, the Chevy II Nova had cemented its position as a formidable competitor in the compact segment. While the design evolution from 1962 to 1965 wasn't revolutionary, it demonstrated Chevrolet's commitment to continuous improvement and refinement. These early years established the foundation for the more dramatic transformation that would follow in the second generation, as the Nova began its metamorphosis from humble compact to legitimate muscle car contender.

Chapter 3: Under the Hood: Engineering Marvels of the Chevy II Nova

Section 3.1: The Heart of the Beast - Nova's Engine Evolution

The Chevy II Nova's journey through automotive history is intrinsically linked to the evolution of its powerplant. From modest beginnings to tire-shredding powerhouses, the Nova's engine options tell a story of American engineering ingenuity and the changing landscape of consumer demands.

In the early 1960s, the Chevy II made its debut with a focus on economy and practicality. The 1962 model year introduced a 153 cubic inch four-cylinder engine, producing a modest 90 horsepower. This engine, while not a powerhouse, was designed for efficiency and reliability, catering to families looking for an affordable and dependable vehicle. Alongside the four-cylinder, Chevrolet offered an inline-six engine option, providing a balance between economy and improved performance for those who desired a bit more pep in their daily driver.

Chevy II Nova: Power, Passion, and Performance

The automotive landscape began to shift dramatically in the mid-1960s, and Chevrolet responded by introducing V8 engines to the Nova lineup. This move transformed the Nova from a purely economical option to a potential performance machine. In 1964, the introduction of the 283 cubic inch V8 engine marked a turning point, boosting the Nova's power output to 195 horsepower. This addition broadened the Nova's appeal, attracting enthusiasts who craved more power without sacrificing the car's compact dimensions.

As the muscle car era reached its zenith in the late 1960s and early 1970s, the Nova's engine options grew increasingly potent. The pinnacle of this evolution came in 1970, when the Nova SS could be equipped with a monstrous 396 cubic-inch big-block V8. This powerplant churned out an impressive 375 horsepower, catapulting the unassuming Nova into the realm of serious performance cars. The combination of high power output in a relatively lightweight chassis made the Nova SS a force to be reckoned with on both the street and the drag strip.

However, the automotive industry's focus began to shift in the mid-1970s due to rising fuel costs and increasing environmental concerns. This change in market demands and stricter regulations led Chevrolet to adjust the Nova's engine lineup once again. By 1976, the largest available engine had been reduced to a 350 cubic inch V8, reflecting the growing emphasis on fuel economy. While still potent, these later engines were designed with a greater focus on efficiency and emissions control.

Throughout its production run, the engineering principles behind Nova's engines remained at the forefront of automotive technology. Chevrolet's engineers utilized advanced casting techniques to create lighter, more efficient engine blocks. They also employed innovative combustion chamber designs and valve train configurations to maximize power output while meeting increasingly stringent emissions standards.

The Nova's engine evolution wasn't just about raw power; it was a testament to Chevrolet's ability to adapt to changing market conditions and technological advancements. From the early inline engines focused on economy to the mid-year V8s that turned the Nova into a performance icon, and finally to the later models that balanced power with efficiency, each iteration showcased the ingenuity of American engineering.

This diverse range of engines allowed the Nova to fill multiple roles in the automotive market. It could be a frugal family car, a weekend racer, or anything in between, depending on the engine choice. This versatility was a key factor in the Nova's enduring popularity and its ability to remain relevant throughout its production run.

The legacy of these engines extends beyond the Nova itself. Many of the technological advancements and engineering lessons learned during the development of Nova's engines influenced the design of future Chevrolet powerplants. The spirit of innovation that drove the constant evolution of the Nova's heart continues to beat in the engines of modern Chevrolet vehicles, a testament to the lasting impact of this iconic model's engineering heritage.

Section 3.2: Transmission and Drivetrain Developments

The Chevy II Nova's evolution wasn't limited to its impressive engine lineup. The transmission and drivetrain components underwent significant developments throughout the vehicle's production run, playing a crucial role in delivering the Nova's power to the pavement.

In its early years, the 1962 Chevy II offered a standard three-speed manual transmission, providing drivers with a direct connection to the powertrain. For those who preferred a more relaxed driving experience, an optional two-speed Powerglide automatic transmission was available. This simple yet effective automatic transmission was well-suited to the modest power output of the early Nova engines, offering smooth shifts and reliable performance for daily driving.

As the Nova's engine options grew more powerful, so too did the need for more robust and performance-oriented transmissions. In 1968, Chevrolet introduced a heavy-duty four-speed manual transmission option, perfectly complementing the Nova's increasingly muscular V8 engines. This transmission allowed drivers to extract maximum performance from their vehicles, with closer gear ratios and a more direct feel that appealed to enthusiasts and racers alike.

The automatic transmission options also saw significant improvements over time. The introduction of the three-speed Turbo-Hydramatic in 1969 marked a substantial upgrade in the Nova's automatic transmission performance. This transmission offered smoother shifts, better durability, and improved efficiency compared to the older Powerglide. The Turbo-Hydramatic was well-equipped to handle the increased torque of the larger V8 engines, making it a popular choice for both performance and comfort-oriented Nova buyers.

An often-overlooked but crucial component of the Nova's drivetrain was its rear axle. Chevrolet offered a range of rear axle ratios to suit different driving preferences and performance goals. For everyday drivers focused on fuel economy, a numerically lower ratio like 2.73:1 was available. However, performance enthusiasts could opt for a much more aggressive 4.11:1 rear axle ratio, dramatically improving acceleration at the cost of fuel efficiency and high-speed cruising comfort. This flexibility allowed Nova owners to tailor their vehicles to their specific needs and driving styles.

The engineering behind the Nova's drivetrain durability was particularly noteworthy. As the power output of Nova engines increased, Chevrolet engineers rose to the challenge of creating a drivetrain that could withstand the additional stress. They reinforced critical components such as the driveshaft and U-joints to handle the increased torque of larger V8 engines. This attention to detail ensured that the Nova's drivetrain remained reliable even under high-stress conditions, contributing to the car's reputation for durability.

Another significant development in Nova's transmission history was the introduction of overdrive gears in later models. These overdrive transmissions, both manual and automatic, enabled lower engine speeds during highway cruising, thereby improving fuel economy and reducing engine wear. This adaptation reflected the shifting priorities of the automotive market, striking a balance between performance and efficiency.

The Nova's transmission and drivetrain developments weren't just about raw performance; they also focused on improving the overall driving experience. Engineers worked to reduce transmission noise and vibration, resulting in a smoother and more refined feel. This was particularly noticeable in later Nova models, which benefited from years of continuous improvement and refinement.

It's worth noting that the Nova's drivetrain components often found their way into other Chevrolet vehicles and even custom hot rods, a testament to their strength and versatility. Many of these parts became favorites among automotive enthusiasts for their durability and performance potential, further cementing the Nova's place in automotive history.

In conclusion, the evolution of the Chevy II Nova's transmission and drivetrain mirrors the car's overall development from a modest compact to a versatile performance machine. From basic three-speed manuals to robust four-speeds, from the simple Powerglide to the advanced Turbo-Hydramatic, these developments played a crucial role in defining the Nova's character and capabilities. The engineering ingenuity behind these components ensured that the Nova could efficiently and reliably transmit its power to the road, regardless of whether it was equipped with an economical six-cylinder or a tire-shredding V8.

Section 3.3: Suspension and Handling Innovations

The Chevy II Nova's reputation as a versatile and capable vehicle was due in no small part to its sophisticated suspension and handling characteristics. From its inception, Chevrolet engineers have focused on creating a balanced and responsive driving experience that appeals to a wide range of customers, from daily commuters to performance enthusiasts.

When the Chevy II Nova first rolled off the production line in 1962, it featured a conventional suspension setup that was both reliable and cost-effective. The front suspension utilized a standard coil spring configuration, while the rear employed a tried-and-true leaf spring system. This basic arrangement provided a comfortable ride for everyday driving while still offering decent handling capabilities for its time.

As the Nova evolved and its performance potential increased, Chevrolet recognized the need for more advanced suspension options. The introduction of the Nova SS package brought with it a host of improvements designed to enhance both ride quality and cornering ability. These upgrades included heavier-duty springs and shocks, which not only improved the car's stability during high-speed maneuvers but also gave the Nova a more planted feel on the road.

The evolution of the Nova's steering systems played a crucial role in its handling characteristics. Early models featured a recirculating ball steering setup, which was typical for the era. However, as technology progressed, so did the Nova's steering. In 1974, Chevrolet introduced a new energy-absorbing steering column to the Nova, significantly improving safety without sacrificing the road feel that drivers had come to appreciate. This innovation demonstrated

Chevrolet's commitment to blending performance with practicality and safety.

As the Nova's engine options grew more potent over the years, the need for improved braking capabilities became evident. Chevrolet engineers rose to the challenge, and in 1971, front disc brakes became standard equipment on all V8-equipped Novas. This upgrade significantly enhanced the car's braking performance, providing drivers with increased confidence and control, particularly when pushing the vehicle to its limits.

The Nova's handling characteristics were not solely the result of individual components, but rather a holistic approach to chassis engineering. Chevrolet's team worked tirelessly to fine-tune the Nova's weight distribution, aiming for a near 50/50 front-to-rear balance. This attention to detail resulted in a car that was remarkably agile for its class, with neutral handling that could satisfy both casual drivers and enthusiasts alike.

Throughout its production run, the Nova benefited from continuous refinements to its suspension geometry. Engineers adjusted factors such as caster, camber, and toe to optimize tire contact with the road, enhancing both grip and tire longevity. These subtle tweaks, often invisible to the casual observer, contributed significantly to the Nova's reputation for predictable and enjoyable handling.

For those seeking the ultimate in handling performance, Chevrolet offered a range of dealer-installed options and factory upgrades. These included sway bars, performance-tuned shocks, and even complete suspension packages designed to transform the Nova into a formidable track machine. This flexibility allowed owners to tailor their Nova's handling characteristics to their specific needs and preferences.

Chevy II Nova: Power, Passion, and Performance

The Nova's suspension and handling innovations weren't limited to performance enhancements. Comfort was also a key consideration, particularly in later models. The introduction of improved bushing materials and isolation techniques helped to reduce noise, vibration, and harshness (NVH), resulting in a smoother and quieter ride without compromising handling prowess.

As emission regulations and fuel economy concerns began to shape the automotive landscape in the 1970s, the Nova's suspension engineers faced new challenges. They had to maintain the car's handling characteristics while accommodating changes in weight distribution due to new engine configurations and emissions equipment. Their success in this endeavor is a testament to the robust and adaptable nature of the Nova's chassis design.

The legacy of the Chevy II Nova's suspension and handling innovations extends far beyond its production years. Many of the lessons learned and techniques developed during the Nova's evolution have influenced Chevrolet's approach to vehicle dynamics in subsequent models. The balance of performance, comfort, and safety achieved in the Nova remains a benchmark for Chevrolet's engineering teams to this day.

In conclusion, the suspension and handling innovations of the Chevy II Nova played a crucial role in establishing its reputation as a versatile and capable vehicle. From its humble beginnings with a conventional setup to the advanced systems of later models, the Nova's suspension engineering demonstrated Chevrolet's commitment to continuous improvement and driver satisfaction. These innovations not only enhanced the Nova's performance but also contributed to its enduring appeal among enthusiasts and collectors, cementing its place in automotive history as a true engineering marvel.

Section 3.4: Body and Chassis Engineering

The Chevy II Nova's body and chassis engineering represented a significant leap forward in automotive design and construction. At the heart of the Nova's engineering marvel was its unibody construction, a departure from the traditional body-on-frame design used in many contemporary vehicles. This innovative approach provided increased structural rigidity while simultaneously reducing overall weight compared to its full-size counterparts. The unibody design not only improved the Nova's handling characteristics but also contributed to better fuel efficiency and a more responsive driving experience.

As the Nova evolved through its production years, Chevrolet engineers continually refined the body and chassis design to incorporate new materials and manufacturing techniques. Later Nova models, for instance, utilized galvanized steel panels in key areas prone to corrosion. This forward-thinking approach significantly improved the vehicle's longevity, addressing one of the most common issues faced by car owners of the era. The use of galvanized steel was just one example of how Chevrolet stayed ahead of the curve in terms of materials science and its application in automotive manufacturing.

Aerodynamics played an increasingly important role in the Nova's design as the years progressed. The 1968 redesign, in particular, showcased Chevrolet's growing awareness of the importance of aerodynamic efficiency. The new model featured a more sloped roofline, which not only gave the car a more modern appearance but also reduced drag and improved high-speed stability. This attention to aerodynamic detail was relatively rare in the compact car segment at the time, demonstrating Chevrolet's commitment to performance across all aspects of the vehicle's design.

One of the less visible but equally important aspects of the Nova's body and chassis engineering was its focus on reducing noise, vibration, and harshness (NVH). Chevrolet engineers employed a variety of techniques to improve ride quality and interior comfort. Strategically placed sound-deadening materials were used to reduce road noise and engine vibration, resulting in a quieter, more refined driving experience. This attention to NVH engineering set the Nova apart from many of its competitors, offering a level of refinement typically associated with more expensive vehicles.

Safety engineering was another area where the Nova showcased significant advancements throughout its production run. As federal safety standards evolved, so did the Nova's safety features. The 1973 model year saw the introduction of a new impact-absorbing front bumper system, designed to meet new federal safety standards. This system not only improved the vehicle's ability to withstand low-speed collisions but also integrated seamlessly with the Nova's overall design aesthetic.

The Nova's chassis design also underwent continuous refinement to improve handling and ride quality. Engineers fine-tuned the suspension mounting points and chassis reinforcements to achieve an optimal balance between comfort and performance. This meticulous approach to chassis tuning resulted in a vehicle that was equally at home cruising on the highway or carving through twisty back roads.

Chevrolet's commitment to quality in the Nova's body and chassis engineering extended to the manufacturing process as well. Advanced welding techniques and precision assembly processes ensured that each Nova left the factory with consistent build quality. This attention to detail in the manufacturing process contributed significantly to the Nova's reputation for reliability and longevity.

The Nova's body and chassis engineering also allowed for remarkable flexibility in terms of powertrain options. The robust unibody design could accommodate everything from economical inline-four engines to powerful big-block V8s without requiring significant structural modifications. This versatility was a key factor in the Nova's broad appeal and its ability to serve as a platform for everything from basic transportation to high-performance muscle cars.

In conclusion, the body and chassis engineering of the Chevy II Nova represented a harmonious blend of innovation, practicality, and performance. From its pioneering unibody construction to its advanced safety features and refined NVH characteristics, the Nova showcased Chevrolet's engineering prowess. This solid foundation not only contributed to the Nova's success during its production run but also cemented its place as a beloved classic in automotive history.

Section 3.5: Fuel and Emissions Systems

The evolution of fuel and emissions systems in the Chevy II Nova reflects not only the changing landscape of automotive technology but also the increasing awareness of environmental concerns throughout its production run. From simple carburetors to advanced fuel injection systems, the Nova's fuel delivery methods underwent significant transformations, each bringing improvements in performance, efficiency, and cleanliness.

In its early years, the Nova relied on straightforward carburetion systems. The 1962 Chevy II, for instance, utilized a single-barrel carburetor on its four-cylinder engine, while the six-cylinder received a two-barrel setup. These simple yet effective systems were well-suited to the modest power outputs of the early models, providing adequate fuel delivery for everyday driving conditions.

As the Nova's performance potential grew, so did the sophistication of its fuel delivery systems. The introduction of V8 engines brought with it more advanced carburetion options. High-performance Nova models could be equipped with a Holley four-barrel carburetor, dramatically improving fuel delivery under heavy acceleration. This upgrade was particularly popular among enthusiasts who sought to maximize their Nova's power output.

The carburetor remained the primary fuel delivery method for most of the Nova's production run, but it didn't stay static. Engineers continually refined carburetor designs, improving fuel atomization, throttle response, and fuel efficiency. Innovations, such as vacuum-operated secondary barrels and adjustable metering rods, allowed for improved performance across a broader range of driving conditions.

However, the most significant change in the Nova's fuel system came with the introduction of fuel injection. In 1985, the Nova received throttle-body fuel injection, marking a significant leap forward in both performance and fuel efficiency. This system provided more precise fuel metering, improved cold-start performance, and reduced emissions compared to traditional carburetors.

As emissions regulations became increasingly stringent throughout the 1970s and 1980s, Chevrolet engineers faced the challenge of maintaining the Nova's performance while meeting new environmental standards. The 1975 Nova introduced a catalytic converter, significantly reducing harmful exhaust emissions. This addition, while necessary for compliance, initially posed challenges for performance enthusiasts.

To address these challenges, engineers developed innovative solutions. A unique exhaust gas recirculation (EGR) system was designed to reduce emissions without significantly impacting engine output. This system worked by recirculating a portion of the exhaust gases back into the combustion chamber, lowering peak combustion temperatures and reducing the formation of nitrogen oxides.

The implementation of computer-controlled engine management systems in later Nova models further improved the balance between performance and emissions compliance. These systems enabled more precise control of fuel delivery and ignition timing, thereby optimizing engine operation across diverse driving conditions.

Despite these advancements, the transition to cleaner-running engines was not without its challenges. Early emissions control systems often resulted in decreased power output and reduced fuel efficiency. However, as technology progressed, engineers found ways to mitigate these drawbacks, eventually producing engines that were both cleaner and more powerful than their predecessors.

The Nova's journey from simple carburetors to sophisticated fuel injection and emissions control systems mirrors the broader evolution of automotive technology in the late 20th century. Each advancement brought new capabilities and challenges, pushing engineers to innovate and adapt. The result was a car that remained relevant and competitive throughout its long production run, capable of meeting the changing demands of both consumers and regulators.

Today, the various fuel and emissions systems used throughout the Nova's history provide a fascinating study for enthusiasts and restorers. From the simplicity of early carburetors to the complexity of late-model fuel injection systems, each iteration tells a story of engineering progress and adaptation to changing times. The Nova's ability to evolve in this crucial area was key to its enduring success and continues to be a point of interest for those who appreciate the engineering behind this iconic American automobile.

Section 3.6: Electrical and Ignition Systems

The Chevy II Nova's electrical and ignition systems underwent significant evolution throughout its production run, reflecting the rapid advancements in automotive technology during this period. In its early years, the Nova featured a basic yet reliable electrical system that laid the foundation for future innovations.

Chevy II Nova: Power, Passion, and Performance

The 1962 Chevy II debuted with a straightforward 12-volt electrical system, which was standard for vehicles of its era. This system utilized a generator for charging, providing adequate power for the car's modest electrical needs. However, as the Nova's features and performance capabilities expanded, so too did the demands on its electrical system.

A significant milestone in Nova's electrical evolution came in 1963 with the introduction of an alternator charging system. This upgrade represented a major improvement over the previous generator setup. Alternators provided more consistent electrical output across all engine speeds, ensuring a stable power supply even when the engine was idling. This was particularly beneficial for Nova models equipped with power-hungry accessories or high-performance engines that required more electrical current.

The Nova's ignition system also saw substantial advancements over the years. Early models employed a traditional points-style ignition, which was effective but required regular maintenance. As technology progressed, Chevrolet engineers sought ways to improve the Nova's ignition reliability and performance. In 1975, they introduced an optional High Energy Ignition (HEI) system, which marked a significant leap forward in ignition technology.

The HEI system provided a hotter, more consistent spark, resulting in improved engine performance, fuel economy, and cold-weather starting. This system was also more reliable and required less maintenance than its predecessors, making it a popular option among Nova owners. The HEI system's success led to its widespread adoption across the Chevrolet lineup, cementing its place as a landmark innovation in automotive ignition technology.

As the automotive industry entered the computer age, the Nova kept pace with the integration of electronic controls. The introduction of the Computer Command Control (CCC) system in 1981 revolutionized the Nova's engine management. This system utilized sensors and a central processing unit to precisely control fuel delivery and ignition timing, resulting in improved performance, enhanced fuel efficiency, and reduced emissions. The CCC system represented a significant step towards the sophisticated engine management systems found in modern vehicles.

The Nova's lighting and accessory electrical systems also saw continuous improvement throughout its production run. Later models featured solid-state voltage regulators, which improved the reliability of the electrical system as a whole. This upgrade ensured more stable voltage for all of the car's electrical components, reducing wear and extending the life of bulbs, motors, and other electrical accessories.

Advancements in the Nova's gauge cluster and instrument panel reflected the car's overall electrical evolution. Early models featured simple analog gauges, but as the years progressed, more sophisticated instrumentation was introduced. Some later Nova models offered optional digital displays for speed and engine information, showcasing Chevrolet's commitment to incorporating cutting-edge technology into their vehicles.

The electrical system's capacity also grew to accommodate the increasing number of power accessories available on the Nova. Features like power windows, locks, and seats, which were once rare luxuries, became more common in later Nova models. This required a more robust electrical system capable of handling these additional loads without compromising performance or reliabllity.

Throughout its production run, the Nova's electrical and ignition systems demonstrated Chevrolet's ability to adapt to changing technology and consumer demands. From its humble beginnings with a basic generator and points ignition to its later iterations with computer-controlled engine management, the Nova's electrical evolution mirrored the rapid advancement of automotive technology in the latter half of the 20th century.

These electrical and ignition system improvements not only enhanced the Nova's performance and reliability but also contributed to its longevity as a popular choice among car enthusiasts. The robust and adaptable nature of these systems allowed the Nova to remain relevant and competitive, even as newer models entered the market. Today, the electrical innovations pioneered in vehicles like the Nova continue to influence modern automotive design, serving as a testament to the enduring legacy of this iconic American automobile.

Section 3.7: Comparative Analysis

When examining the Chevy II Nova's engineering prowess, it's essential to consider how it stacked up against its contemporaries. This comparative analysis provides valuable insights into Nova's strengths and innovations within the competitive landscape of its era.

In the realm of engine offerings, the Nova consistently provided a diverse range of options that often outpaced its rivals. While the Ford Falcon and Plymouth Valiant offered respectable powerplants, the Nova's engine lineup frequently boasted superior power-to-weight ratios. For instance, when equipped with the potent 396 cubic inch V8, the Nova SS could outmuscle many of its competitors in straight-line acceleration. The Nova's inline-six engines were particularly noteworthy, offering better low-end torque than the slant-six found in Plymouth's offerings, resulting in more responsive everyday driving characteristics.

Suspension and handling characteristics were areas where the Nova truly shone. The Nova SS, with its performance-tuned suspension, consistently outperformed rivals like the Dodge Dart in road tests. Automotive journalists of the time frequently praised the Nova's balanced handling and predictable road manners, especially in its performance-oriented configurations. This superiority in handling wasn't limited to just the SS models; even standard Novas were often lauded for their composed ride quality and responsive steering, making them popular choices for both daily driving and weekend cruising.

When it comes to build quality and durability, the Nova earned a reputation for longevity that set it apart from many of its contemporaries. Numerous Nova owners reported their vehicles reaching high mileage with minimal issues, often outlasting comparable models from other manufacturers. This durability was a testament to Chevrolet's engineering and manufacturing processes, which prioritized robust construction and reliable components. The Nova's unibody construction, introduced from the outset, provided a rigid platform that contributed to its long-term durability and resistance to structural fatigue.

In terms of innovative features, the Nova often led the pack in its segment. The optional disc brakes available on the Nova were frequently praised for their superior stopping power compared to the drum brakes still standard on many competitors. This advantage in braking performance was particularly noteworthy given the increasing power outputs of vehicles during this era. Additionally, the Nova's adoption of advanced ignition systems, such as the High Energy Ignition (HEI) system in later models, provided more consistent performance and improved fuel economy compared to traditional points-style ignition systems still used by some rivals.

The Nova's adaptability to different market segments was another area where it outshone many competitors. Its platform could be configured to serve as an economical family car, a comfortable mid-size cruiser, or a high-performance muscle machine. This versatility was a significant engineering achievement, allowing Chevrolet to appeal to a broad range of consumers with a single model line. Few competitors could match the Nova's ability to span such diverse market segments without compromising performance or reliability.

Chevy II Nova: Power, Passion, and Performance

In the realm of fuel efficiency, particularly in later years as emissions regulations tightened, the Nova managed to maintain a competitive edge. The introduction of technologies like throttle-body fuel injection allowed the Nova to achieve better fuel economy than many of its carbureted rivals while still delivering satisfying performance. This balance of efficiency and power was a testament to Chevrolet's engineering acumen in adapting to changing market demands and regulatory requirements.

While the Nova certainly had its strong points, it's important to note that it wasn't superior in every aspect. Some competitors offered more modern styling in certain model years, and others may have had advantages in specific niche areas. However, when viewed holistically, the Nova's engineering often placed it at or near the top of its class in many crucial aspects of automotive design and performance.

In conclusion, this comparative analysis underscores the Nova's position as a well-engineered, versatile, and often class-leading vehicle of its time. Its combination of powerful engines, adept handling, durability, and innovative features frequently gave it an edge over its competitors. The Nova's ability to compete strongly across various metrics is a testament to the skill and foresight of Chevrolet's engineering teams, cementing the Nova's place as a significant player in automotive history.

Chapter 4: The Nova in Pop Culture: A Symbol of American Automotive Prowess

Section 4.1: The Nova on the Silver Screen

The Chevrolet Nova's journey from dealership showrooms to Hollywood stardom is a testament to its enduring appeal and cultural significance. As a versatile and visually striking vehicle, the Nova has graced the silver screen in numerous memorable appearances, cementing its status as an iconic American automobile.

In major Hollywood films, the Nova has often been cast in roles that highlight its power, style, and cultural associations. One notable example is its appearance in Quentin Tarantino's "Death Proof" (2007). In this film, the Nova is not just a background prop but a central character in its own right. Stuntman Mike, played by Kurt Russell, drives a menacing black 1971 Chevy Nova SS, reinforcing the car's image as a muscle car icon. The Nova's presence in this film showcases its raw power and intimidating presence, qualities that have made it a favorite among car enthusiasts and filmmakers alike.

Chevy II Nova: Power, Passion, and Performance

The Nova's portrayal in different film genres demonstrates its versatility as a cinematic symbol. In action films, the car often represents rugged individualism and unbridled power. Its compact size, coupled with potent engine options, makes it an ideal choice for high-speed chases and daring stunts. Conversely, in coming-of-age dramas or period pieces set in the 1960s and 1970s, the Nova frequently serves as a symbol of youth, freedom, and the changing social landscape of America.

Car chase scenes have been a staple of action movies for decades, and the Nova has played its part in some of the most thrilling sequences. The adrenaline-pumping chase in "Terminator 2: Judgment Day" (1991) is a prime example. Although not the primary vehicle in the scene, the Nova's appearance showcases its speed and agility, holding its own against more modern cars. This scene not only entertained audiences but also reinforced the Nova's reputation as a formidable street machine.

Beyond blockbuster action films, the Nova has also left its mark on cult classics. Its appearance in Richard Linklater's "Dazed and Confused" (1993) is particularly noteworthy. Set in the 1970s, the film features several Novas, using the car to evoke nostalgia and capture the essence of the era. This association with 1970s youth culture has further cemented the Nova's place in the American collective memory, making it a go-to choice for filmmakers seeking to recreate the look and feel of this pivotal decade.

The Nova's influence extends beyond its on-screen appearances to real-world car customization. Movies featuring modified Novas have inspired enthusiasts to replicate these designs, creating a feedback loop between cinema and car culture. The "Fast and Furious" franchise, while not exclusively featuring Novas, has had a significant impact on car modification trends. The street racing culture depicted in these films has led many Nova owners to modify their vehicles for enhanced performance and style, mirroring the on-screen aesthetics.

In conclusion, the Nova's presence on the silver screen has been far more than mere product placement. It has become a character in its own right, capable of conveying complex ideas about American culture, power, and individuality. From high-octane action sequences to nostalgic period pieces, the Nova's versatility as a cinematic symbol has ensured its place in film history. This on-screen legacy continues to influence how the car is perceived and appreciated in the real world, making the Nova not just a part of automotive history but a true icon of American popular culture.

Section 4.2: The Nova in Television

The Chevrolet Nova's influence extended far beyond the silver screen, making its mark on television screens across America and worldwide. Popular TV shows frequently featured the Nova, cementing its status as a quintessential American car of the era. One notable example is its appearance in "That '70s Show," where it served as a perfect representation of the decade's automotive culture, reinforcing its place in the collective memory of American viewers.

The Nova's appeal wasn't limited to scripted television. Automotive enthusiasts recognized the car's enduring popularity and dedicated significant airtime to showcasing its potential. Programs like "Overhaulin'" devoted entire episodes to Nova restorations, highlighting the car's timeless appeal and the passion it evokes in car lovers. These shows not only entertained but also educated viewers on the Nova's history, mechanics, and customization possibilities, inspiring a new generation of enthusiasts.

Television commercials played a crucial role in shaping the Nova's public image over the years. Chevrolet's marketing strategies evolved alongside the car, reflecting changing societal values and consumer preferences. In the 1960s, TV ads for the Nova emphasized its compact size and affordability, appealing to budget-conscious families and first-time car buyers. As the decade progressed and the Nova gained more powerful engine options, commercials began to highlight its performance capabilities, aligning with the growing muscle car trend.

The Nova's significance in automotive history has been recognized by numerous educational programs and documentaries. The History Channel's "Modern Marvels" series, known for its in-depth exploration of technological advancements, featured the Nova prominently in its episode on muscle cars. This coverage provided viewers with a comprehensive look at the Nova's evolution from a modest compact to a powerful performance machine, contextualizing its importance in the broader narrative of American automotive innovation.

Interestingly, the Nova's influence wasn't confined to American television. Its appearances on international shows introduced the car to audiences worldwide, creating a global fanbase. The British show "Top Gear," renowned for its humorous and often irreverent take on car culture, featured the Nova in several episodes. This exposure introduced the quintessentially American car to a new generation of international enthusiasts, sparking interest and admiration for American automotive design and engineering beyond U.S. borders.

From entertainment to education, from national broadcasts to international airwaves, the Chevrolet Nova has left an indelible mark on television history. Its frequent appearances across various TV formats have not only reflected its popularity but also played a significant role in shaping public perception of the car. Through television, the Nova has transcended its role as a mere vehicle to become a cultural icon, representing an era of American automotive prowess and innovation that continues to captivate audiences worldwide.

Section 4.3: The Nova in Music

The Chevrolet Nova's influence extends far beyond the automotive world, leaving an indelible mark on the music industry.

Chevy II Nova: Power, Passion, and Performance

This iconic vehicle has found its way into song lyrics, music videos, album artwork, and even inspired musicians themselves, cementing its status as a symbol of American car culture in popular music.

References to the Nova in song lyrics have been numerous and diverse, spanning multiple genres and decades. Musicians have often used the Nova as a symbol of freedom, youth, and rebellion. The Beach Boys, known for their car-centric lyrics, famously alluded to the Nova's engine options in their hit "I Get Around" with the line "my four-speed, dual-quad, Posi-Traction 409." This reference not only showcased the Nova's performance capabilities but also highlighted its popularity among young car enthusiasts of the era.

The Nova's visual appeal has made it a staple in music videos, where it often serves as a powerful symbol of Americana and vintage cool. Its sleek lines and muscular stance have graced countless music videos, adding a touch of nostalgia and automotive flair. A prime example is Lana Del Rey's "Born to Die" video, where the Nova's presence reinforces the song's themes of vintage Americana and youthful rebellion. The car's appearance in this and other videos has helped introduce the Nova to newer generations, ensuring its continued cultural relevance.

While the Nova itself may not have graced many album covers directly, its influence on album artwork is undeniable. The hot rod culture that the Nova helped popularize has been a recurring theme in album design, particularly in rock and country music. ZZ Top's iconic "Eliminator" album cover, featuring a customized Ford, inspired many Nova owners to emulate the hot rod style on their own vehicles. This cross-pollination between music and car culture has kept the Nova at the forefront of automotive enthusiasm.

Several high-profile musicians have been known for their love of Novas, further boosting the car's cultural cache. Jay Leno, former late-night host and renowned car collector, has featured his meticulously restored Nova on his show "Jay Leno's Garage." This exposure to millions of viewers has helped maintain interest in the Nova and classic car restoration in general. Other celebrities' associations with the Nova have ranged from using them in performances to collecting and restoring them as a hobby, each instance reinforcing the car's cool factor.

The Nova's influence on car culture in music extends beyond direct references. Its association with street racing and customization culture has shaped automotive themes in various musical genres, notably in hip-hop. Numerous tracks about car customization, speed, and street credibility draw inspiration from the culture surrounding cars, such as the Nova. This influence has created a feedback loop between music and car culture, with each continually inspiring and reshaping the other.

The Nova's musical legacy isn't confined to a single era or genre. From 1960s surf rock to contemporary hip-hop, the car has maintained its cultural relevance. It has been name-dropped in country songs as a symbol of small-town America, featured in rock anthems as an emblem of rebellion, and celebrated in rap lyrics as a classic ride worthy of respect.

This enduring presence in music has helped the Nova transcend its status as merely a car, transforming it into a cultural icon. Through music, the Nova has come to represent not just a mode of transportation, but a lifestyle, an era, and a distinctly American spirit of freedom and innovation. As long as musicians continue to celebrate the allure of the open road and the power of American engineering, the Nova will likely maintain its place in the soundtrack of our lives.

Section 4.4: The Nova in Literature and Print Media

The Chevrolet Nova's influence extends far beyond the realms of film, television, and music. It has also left an indelible mark on literature and print media, cementing its status as a cultural icon. From novels to comic books, and from magazines to advertisements, the Nova has been a recurring motif that captures the imagination of writers, artists, and readers alike.

In the world of literature, the Nova has made numerous appearances, often serving as more than just a mode of transportation for characters. While Stephen King's "Christine" famously featured a possessed Plymouth Fury, it inspired a wave of horror stories featuring possessed Novas. These tales tapped into the car's muscle and power, transforming it into a vehicle of supernatural terror. In other novels and short stories, the Nova frequently symbolizes freedom, rebellion, or the quintessential American dream. Its presence in narratives often evokes a sense of nostalgia for the 1960s and 1970s, a time of significant cultural and social change in America.

The visual world of comic books and graphic novels has also embraced the Nova. Artists have lovingly rendered the car's sleek lines and powerful stance, using it to enhance their storytelling. In Marvel Comics, for instance, the Nova often appears as the everyday hero's reliable transportation, subtly reinforcing the character's relatability and down-to-earth nature. The car's appearance in these visual media has helped to immortalize its design, allowing new generations to appreciate its aesthetic appeal.

There may be no doubt that Nova's presence has been more consistent and influential than in automotive magazines. Publications like Hot Rod Magazine, Car Craft, and Super Chevy have featured countless Nova project cars, restorations, and modifications over the years. These detailed articles and vibrant photo spreads have inspired countless readers to start their own Nova projects, fueling a community of enthusiasts and preserving the car's legacy. The Nova's regular appearance in these magazines has also helped to document its evolution, from its early days as an economy car to its later status as a sought-after collector's item.

In the realm of advertising, the Nova has been a powerful tool for Chevrolet to communicate its brand values. Print advertisements featuring the Nova often emphasized its versatility, affordability, and all-American appeal. The iconic "Baseball, Hot Dogs, Apple Pie and Chevrolet" campaign frequently showcased the Nova alongside other Chevrolet models, cementing its place in the pantheon of classic American cars. These advertisements, now collectors' items in their own right, offer a fascinating glimpse into how the Nova was marketed and perceived throughout its production run.

The Nova has also captured the imagination of automotive photographers, who have used their lenses to elevate the car to an art form. Renowned automotive photographer Larry Chen, for example, has created stunning Nova shoots that highlight the car's timeless design and cultural significance. These artistic interpretations of the Nova have helped to maintain its allure, even as the automotive landscape has changed dramatically since its heyday.

The Nova's enduring presence in literature and print media speaks to its versatility as a cultural symbol. Whether it's being used to evoke a specific era, represent American ingenuity, or simply showcase automotive beauty, the Nova continues to captivate writers, artists, and readers. This persistent appeal in print has played a crucial role in maintaining the Nova's status as an icon of American automotive culture, ensuring that its legacy will continue to inspire future generations of car enthusiasts and storytellers alike.

Section 4.5: The Nova in Digital Media and Video Games

The Chevrolet Nova's influence extends far beyond the physical realm, making significant inroads into the digital landscape. As technology has advanced, so too has the Nova's presence in various digital media formats, particularly in video games. This digital representation has played a crucial role in introducing the classic car to new generations of enthusiasts and maintaining its relevance in contemporary car culture.

Chevy II Nova: Power, Passion, and Performance

Racing video games have been at the forefront of featuring the Nova in digital environments. Popular franchises like Forza have included various models of the Nova, allowing players to experience the car's power and handling in a virtual setting. These games often feature meticulously detailed recreations of the Nova, from its iconic body lines to the rumble of its engine. The ability to customize and upgrade these virtual Novas has also sparked interest in real-world modifications among players.

In open-world video games, the Nova often appears as a symbol of a specific era or aesthetic. Games like the Grand Theft Auto series frequently include cars inspired by the Nova, using them to evoke the atmosphere of 1960s and 1970s America. These appearances help cement the Nova's status as a cultural icon, recognizable even to those who may never have seen one in person.

The rise of social media and online communities has provided Nova enthusiasts with unprecedented opportunities to connect and share their passion. Facebook groups like "Chevy Nova Enthusiasts" boast thousands of members who regularly share restoration tips, parts for sale, and personal stories about their Novas. These online communities have become invaluable resources for Nova owners, fostering a sense of camaraderie and shared experience among enthusiasts worldwide.

YouTube and other video-sharing platforms have also played a significant role in popularizing the Nova in the digital age. Automotive vloggers and content creators often feature Nova restorations, modifications, and reviews in their videos. For example, the popular YouTuber ChrisFix's series on Nova restoration has garnered millions of views, inspiring DIY mechanics and introducing the car to a new audience of potential enthusiasts.

The Nova's digital presence extends to mobile apps and digital tools as well. Apps like "Classic Car VIN Decoder" have become essential for Nova buyers, helping them authenticate potential purchases and understand the history of specific vehicles. Other apps provide maintenance schedules, parts catalogs, and community forums specifically for Nova owners, making it easier than ever to keep these classic cars on the road.

Virtual and augmented reality technologies are also beginning to feature the Nova, allowing enthusiasts to experience the car in new and exciting ways. Some automotive museums have started using VR to let visitors "sit" in classic Novas, while AR apps allow users to visualize how a Nova might look in their driveway.

The Nova's presence in digital media and video games has had a profound impact on its cultural legacy. By making the car accessible in virtual formats, these technologies have helped maintain interest in the Nova among younger generations. They've also provided a platform for preserving the car's history and technical details, ensuring that knowledge about the Nova continues to be passed down.

Moreover, the digital realm has allowed for creative expressions of Nova's enthusiasm that weren't possible before. From digital art featuring the Nova to online Nova-centric events and meetups, the internet has expanded how fans can engage with and celebrate this iconic vehicle.

As technology continues to evolve, Nova's digital presence will only grow stronger. Whether through more advanced gaming engines that provide hyper-realistic driving experiences or through new social platforms that connect enthusiasts in innovative ways, the digital world ensures that the Chevy Nova will continue to captivate car lovers for generations to come.

Section 4.6: The Nova as a Cultural Icon

The Chevrolet Nova has transcended its role as a mere automobile to become a true cultural icon, embodying the spirit of American ingenuity and reflecting the nation's evolving values over decades. This section explores the various ways in which the Nova has left an indelible mark on American culture and beyond.

At its core, the Nova serves as a powerful representation of American car culture. Its journey from an economy car to a muscle car powerhouse mirrors the trajectory of post-World War II America. As the nation experienced unprecedented economic growth and prosperity, consumer desires shifted from basic transportation to vehicles that offered performance and style. The Nova's evolution perfectly encapsulates this change, symbolizing the American dream of constant improvement and the pursuit of power and freedom.

The Nova's influence extends beyond the automotive world, seeping into fashion and style. Vintage-inspired fashion brands frequently incorporate Nova imagery to evoke the essence of 1960s and '70s Americana. T-shirts featuring classic Nova designs, accessories adorned with Nova emblems, and even high-end fashion shoots using the Nova as a backdrop all speak to the car's enduring aesthetic appeal. This fusion of automotive design and fashion underscores the Nova's status as more than just a vehicle; it's a style statement.

In the realm of car customization, the Nova has played a pivotal role. Its lightweight body and adaptable chassis made it an ideal platform for modifications, giving birth to the "sleeper" car culture. Enthusiasts would drop big-block engines into seemingly stock Novas, creating vehicles with surprising performance capabilities. This trend not only showcased American ingenuity but also reflected a cultural appreciation for hidden potential and the thrill of defying expectations.

The Nova also serves as a powerful catalyst for nostalgia and retro appreciation. Events like the "Nova Nationals" attract thousands of enthusiasts each year, celebrating the car's enduring legacy. These gatherings are more than just car shows; they're cultural phenomena where multiple generations come together to share stories, memories, and a mutual appreciation for automotive history. The Nova's ability to evoke nostalgia for different eras, be it the innocence of the early '60s or the rebellious spirit of the '70s, demonstrates its unique position in the American cultural landscape.

Interestingly, the Nova's cultural impact isn't limited to American borders. In Brazil, where the car was sold as the Chevrolet Opala, it has achieved legendary status in local car culture. This international appeal speaks to the universal nature of the Nova's design and the global reach of American automotive culture. From the streets of São Paulo to the highways of California, the Nova's distinctive silhouette is recognized and revered.

The Nova's role as a cultural icon also reflects broader societal themes. Its transformation from an economical family car to a powerful muscle machine mirrors the social changes of the 1960s and '70s, including the rise of youth culture and the challenge to established norms. The Nova became a symbol of freedom and rebellion for a generation coming of age in a time of significant social upheaval.

In the world of collectors and enthusiasts, the Nova holds a special place. Its accessibility, being more affordable than some other classic muscle cars, has made it a popular entry point for newcomers to the classic car hobby. This democratization of classic car ownership has helped keep automotive enthusiasm alive and vibrant, passing the torch to new generations of car lovers.

As we look to the future, the Nova's status as a cultural icon seems secure. In an era of increasing automotive electrification and autonomy, cars like the Nova serve as tangible links to a bygone era of mechanical simplicity and raw power. They remind us of a time when the connection between driver and machine was direct and visceral, evoking a sense of nostalgia even among those too young to have experienced the Nova in its heyday.

In conclusion, the Chevrolet Nova's role as a cultural icon extends far beyond its mechanical specifications or sales figures. It embodies a particular moment in American history, represents the spirit of customization and personal expression, and continues to inspire passion and nostalgia across generations and borders. The Nova is not just a car; it's a cultural touchstone that tells a story of America itself, its dreams, its innovations, and its enduring love affair with the automobile.

Section 4.7: The Nova's Legacy in Pop Culture

The Chevrolet Nova's journey through American pop culture is a testament to its enduring appeal and significance. As we explore the car's legacy, we see how its representation has evolved, reflecting changing societal values and automotive trends.

The Nova's cultural representation has undergone a fascinating transformation since its inception. In the 1960s, it symbolized youth rebellion and the democratization of performance, allowing everyday Americans to access muscle car thrills at an affordable price point. Movies and TV shows of the era often featured Novas as the vehicles of choice for young, rebellious characters. As the decades progressed, the Nova's image shifted. By the 1980s and 1990s, it had become a nostalgic icon, evoking memories of a bygone era of American automotive dominance. Today, the Nova occupies a unique position in pop culture, simultaneously representing vintage Americana and serving as a canvas for modern customization and performance upgrades.

The Nova's influence extends beyond its own model line, inspiring subsequent car designs and shaping the broader automotive landscape. Its compact muscle car formula, which combined a lightweight body with potent V8 engines, influenced designs like the Ford Maverick and Plymouth Duster. Even modern performance cars owe a debt to the Nova's pioneering spirit, with many manufacturers still adhering to the "small car, big engine" philosophy that the Nova helped popularize.

In preserving automotive history, the Nova plays a crucial role. As a bridge between the economic compacts of the early 1960s and the muscle car era, it tells a unique story of American automotive evolution. Museums and car shows frequently feature Novas to illustrate this pivotal period in car culture. The Nova's presence in these settings helps educate new generations about the rich history of American automobiles and the industry's impact on society.

The Nova's impact on automotive enthusiasm cannot be overstated. It continues to inspire new generations of car lovers, often serving as an entry point into the world of classic car restoration and modification. Young enthusiasts who first encounter the Nova through video games or social media usually find themselves drawn to real-world projects, breathing new life into these classic machines. This generational bridge ensures that the Nova's legacy will continue for years to come.

Looking to the future, the Nova's cultural significance is likely to evolve further. As the automotive industry shifts towards electric vehicles and autonomous driving, cars like the Nova may come to symbolize a bygone era of American automotive engineering. However, rather than diminishing its importance, this transition may elevate the Nova's status as a cultural artifact, representing the pinnacle of traditional combustion engine technology and hands-on driving experience.

The Nova's ability to adapt to changing cultural narratives while maintaining its core appeal is its most remarkable legacy. Whether it's being featured in a blockbuster movie, restored on a popular YouTube channel, or showcased at a local car meet, the Nova continues to captivate audiences across generations and platforms. It stands as a symbol of American ingenuity, a testament to the enduring appeal of classic design, and a reminder of the profound impact that automobiles have had on our culture.

As we look back on the Nova's journey through pop culture, we see more than just a car. We know a vehicle that has carried the dreams, aspirations, and memories of generations of Americans. From its humble beginnings as a compact economy car to its current status as a highly sought-after classic, the Chevrolet Nova has carved out a unique place in the cultural landscape. Its legacy serves as a bridge between past and present, connecting car enthusiasts across generations and ensuring that the spirit of American automotive innovation will continue to inspire for years to come.

Chapter 5: Chevrolet's Rising Star: How the Nova Shaped the Brand

Section 5.1: Nova's Strategic Importance to Chevrolet

The Chevy II Nova wasn't just another model in Chevrolet's lineup; it was a strategic masterstroke that significantly impacted the brand's position in the automotive market. As the 1960s dawned, Chevrolet found itself facing a crucial gap in its product offerings. The company's full-size models were selling well, but there was a growing demand for smaller, more economical vehicles that Chevrolet had yet to address effectively. Enter the Nova, a compact car designed to fill this void and compete head-on with Ford's highly successful Falcon and other compact offerings from rival manufacturers.

The Nova's introduction was a clear signal that Chevrolet was not content to rest on its laurels. By swiftly developing and launching the Nova, Chevrolet demonstrated its ability to innovate quickly and respond to changing market conditions. This agility was crucial in an era when consumer preferences were evolving rapidly, and competition in the automotive industry was becoming increasingly fierce.

Chevy II Nova: Power, Passion, and Performance

One of the Nova's key strengths was its appeal to a wide range of demographics. Young families appreciated its affordability and practicality, while first-time car buyers were drawn to its stylish design and reputation for reliability. The Nova also proved popular among older drivers looking to downsize from larger vehicles without sacrificing comfort or quality. This broad appeal allowed Chevrolet to attract new customers to the brand, many of whom would go on to become loyal Chevrolet owners for years to come.

The Nova's success in the compact car segment had a ripple effect across Chevrolet's entire product line. It showcased the brand's ability to compete effectively in multiple market segments, from economy cars to full-size luxury vehicles. This versatility enhanced Chevrolet's image as a forward-thinking automaker capable of meeting diverse consumer needs.

Moreover, the Nova played a crucial role in positioning Chevrolet as a brand that offered value without compromising on quality or performance. The car's balance of affordability, reliability, and style helped reinforce Chevrolet's reputation as "the heartbeat of America," a brand that understood and catered to the needs of everyday Americans.

The strategic importance of the Nova extended beyond its immediate market impact. It served as a platform for Chevrolet to experiment with new technologies and design concepts, many of which would later be incorporated into other models. This spirit of innovation, embodied by the Nova, helped keep Chevrolet at the forefront of automotive development throughout the 1960s and beyond.

In essence, the Nova was more than just a successful model; it was a key component in Chevrolet's broader strategy to maintain its position as one of America's leading automakers. By filling a critical gap in the product line, competing effectively with rival offerings, attracting new demographics, showcasing innovation, and positioning

Chevrolet as a versatile and forward-thinking brand, the Nova played an outsized role in shaping Chevrolet's success during a pivotal period in automotive history.

Section 5.2: Nova's Impact on Chevrolet's Design Philosophy

The introduction of the Chevy II Nova marked a significant shift in Chevrolet's design philosophy, particularly in the realm of compact cars. This new model brought forth a fresh design language that would influence not only its own evolution but also the broader aesthetic direction of the Chevrolet brand.

From its inception, the Nova struck a delicate balance between practicality and style. Its clean lines and uncluttered appearance represented a departure from the more flamboyant designs of the 1950s, signaling Chevrolet's ability to adapt to changing consumer tastes. The Nova's design ethos emphasized functionality without sacrificing visual appeal, a principle that would become increasingly important in Chevrolet's overall design strategy.

As the Nova evolved through its generations, it consistently showcased Chevrolet's ability to stay current with design trends while maintaining its core identity. The early models' boxy yet elegant silhouette gradually gave way to more sculpted and dynamic forms in later years, mirroring broader shifts in automotive design. This adaptability demonstrated Chevrolet's commitment to staying relevant in a rapidly changing market.

The Nova's influence extended beyond its own model line, inspiring design elements in other Chevrolet vehicles. Its emphasis on clean lines and purposeful styling began to appear in larger models, contributing to a more cohesive brand aesthetic across Chevrolet's entire range. This cross-pollination of design ideas helped solidify Chevrolet's image as a forward-thinking automaker with a consistent design language.

Chevy II Nova: Power, Passion, and Performance

One of the Nova's most significant contributions to Chevrolet's design philosophy was its approach to interior design. The Nova set new standards for comfort and functionality in compact cars, proving that smaller vehicles didn't have to sacrifice interior quality or amenities. This focus on creating inviting and well-designed interiors, regardless of vehicle size, became a hallmark of Chevrolet's approach to car design.

The Nova's design also played a crucial role in adapting to changing consumer preferences over time. As market demands shifted from purely functional compact cars to more stylish and performance-oriented vehicles, the Nova's design evolved accordingly. This responsiveness to market trends showcased Chevrolet's ability to read and react to consumer desires, a skill that would prove invaluable in maintaining the brand's relevance and appeal.

Moreover, the Nova's design philosophy emphasized versatility, allowing it to appeal to a wide range of customers. From budget-conscious families to performance enthusiasts, the Nova's adaptable design allowed it to cater to diverse market segments. This versatility in design became a key principle in Chevrolet's broader product strategy, influencing how the brand approached the styling of its entire vehicle lineup.

In essence, the Nova served as a design laboratory for Chevrolet, allowing the brand to experiment with new ideas and refine its aesthetic direction. The lessons learned from the Nova's design journey, the importance of clean lines, the balance of form and function, the need for adaptability, and the value of interior quality all became integral parts of Chevrolet's overarching design philosophy.

The impact of the Nova on Chevrolet's design thinking extended far beyond its production years. It helped establish principles that would guide the brand's aesthetic choices for decades to come, cementing its place not just as a successful model but as a pivotal influence on Chevrolet's design legacy. The Nova proved that thoughtful, adaptable design could be a powerful tool in shaping a brand's identity and connecting with consumers across different eras and market segments.

Section 5.3: Nova's Contribution to Chevrolet's Performance Reputation

The Chevrolet Nova, particularly in its SS (Super Sport) configuration, played a pivotal role in establishing and enhancing Chevrolet's performance reputation during the iconic muscle car era. This unassuming compact car transformed into a powerhouse that left an indelible mark on automotive history and Chevrolet's brand identity.

The introduction of the Nova SS in 1963 marked Chevrolet's entry into the compact performance car segment. With its potent V8 engine options, the Nova SS quickly became a force to be reckoned with on both the streets and the drag strips. This move showcased Chevrolet's commitment to performance across its entire lineup, not just in its larger, more expensive models.

Chevrolet's engine technology took center stage in the Nova SS. The car offered a range of powerful V8 engines, including the legendary 327 and, later, the 350 cubic inch powerplants. These engines weren't just about raw power; they demonstrated Chevrolet's engineering prowess in creating efficient, reliable, and tunable powertrains. The Nova SS became a rolling testament to Chevrolet's ability to pack serious performance into a compact package.

On the drag strips across America, the Nova SS quickly established itself as a formidable competitor. Its combination of lightweight design and potent engines made it a favorite among racers. Victories on the quarter-mile not only brought trophies but also invaluable street credibility to the Chevrolet brand. These wins resonated with young, performance-minded buyers, further cementing Chevrolet's reputation as a maker of serious performance machines.

The Nova SS's success on the strip translated directly to increased interest in the Chevrolet brand among performance enthusiasts. Many who might not have previously considered a Chevrolet found themselves drawn to dealerships, eager to experience the Nova SS's performance firsthand. This influx of enthusiasts didn't just boost Nova sales; it created a halo effect that benefited Chevrolet's entire lineup.

Perhaps most significantly, the Nova's performance success influenced the development of other Chevrolet performance models. The lessons learned from the Nova SS - in terms of engine development, weight distribution, and performance tuning found their way into other iconic Chevrolet models. The Camaro, Chevelle SS, and even the Corvette all benefited from the Nova's performance legacy.

The Nova SS didn't just participate in the muscle car era; it helped define it. By proving that impressive performance could come in a compact, affordable package, it expanded the definition of what a muscle car could be. This legacy continued to influence Chevrolet's performance philosophy long after the original Nova ceased production.

In essence, the Nova, particularly in its SS guise, was instrumental in solidifying Chevrolet's reputation as a brand that offered serious performance to a wide range of consumers. It proved that Chevrolet could compete with the best in the high-performance arena, setting a standard that the brand continues to uphold to this day. The Nova's contribution to Chevrolet's performance reputation was not just significant; it was transformative, helping to shape the brand's identity for decades to come.

Section 5.4: Nova's Role in Chevrolet's Marketing and Advertising

The Chevrolet Nova played a pivotal role in shaping Chevrolet's marketing and advertising strategies throughout its production run. As a versatile and appealing compact car, the Nova provided the perfect canvas for Chevrolet to showcase its ability to cater to diverse consumer segments and emphasize the brand's core values of versatility and value.

Key marketing campaigns featuring the Nova were instrumental in establishing its identity and appeal. One of the most memorable campaigns was the "Mr. Goodwrench and the Heartbeat of America" series, which prominently featured the Nova alongside other Chevrolet models. This campaign effectively positioned the Nova as an integral part of the Chevrolet family, emphasizing its reliability and all-American appeal. Another notable campaign was the "Nova Spirit of America" promotion, which coincided with the United States Bicentennial celebrations in 1976. This campaign not only boosted Nova sales but also reinforced Chevrolet's image as a quintessentially American brand.

Chevrolet's marketing team recognized the Nova's potential to appeal to a wide range of consumer segments, and they crafted targeted campaigns accordingly. For young families, advertisements highlighted the Nova's spacious interior and safety features. Performance enthusiasts were enticed with ads showcasing the Nova SS and its powerful engine options. Budget-conscious buyers were drawn to campaigns that emphasized the Nova's affordability and low maintenance costs. This multi-faceted approach allowed Chevrolet to cast a wide net and attract a diverse customer base to the brand.

The versatility and value of the Nova were consistently emphasized in Chevrolet's marketing materials. Advertisements often focused on the car's ability to serve multiple purposes, from daily commuting to weekend getaways. Taglines such as "Nova: The car that fits your life" and "Nova: More car for your money" reinforced these key selling points. By positioning the Nova as a practical yet stylish choice, Chevrolet was able to appeal to pragmatic consumers without sacrificing the car's aspirational qualities.

Chevrolet strategically used the Nova to enhance its overall brand image. The car's combination of style, performance, and affordability aligned perfectly with Chevrolet's brand values. Marketing materials often presented the Nova alongside other Chevrolet models, creating a cohesive brand image that emphasized the company's diverse product lineup. This approach helped to position Chevrolet as a brand that could meet the needs of any driver, regardless of their preferences or budget.

The Nova's presence in Chevrolet dealerships had a significant impact on sales across the entire product line. As a popular and affordable model, the Nova often served as a gateway car, attracting customers to showrooms where they could then be exposed to other Chevrolet offerings. Dealerships frequently used the Nova as a centerpiece in their displays, leveraging its broad appeal to draw in a wide range of potential buyers. This strategy not only boosted Nova sales but also increased foot traffic and interest in other Chevrolet models.

In addition to traditional advertising methods, Chevrolet also utilized the Nova in innovative marketing initiatives. The company sponsored Nova-centric events, such as owner meetups and car shows, fostering a sense of community among Nova enthusiasts. These events not only strengthened brand loyalty but also generated positive word-of-mouth marketing. Chevrolet also leveraged the Nova's popularity in motorsports, particularly drag racing, to enhance its performance credentials and appeal to automotive enthusiasts.

The Nova's role in Chevrolet's marketing and advertising efforts extended beyond just selling cars. It helped to reshape and reinforce Chevrolet's brand identity, positioning the company as a manufacturer of versatile, value-driven vehicles that could appeal to a broad spectrum of American consumers. The lessons learned from marketing the Nova, particularly in terms of targeting diverse demographics and emphasizing versatility, would go on to influence Chevrolet's advertising strategies for years to come, leaving an indelible mark on the brand's approach to consumer engagement and perception management.

Section 5.5: Nova's Influence on Chevrolet's Manufacturing and Quality Control

The Chevy II Nova didn't just reshape Chevrolet's product lineup; it also had a profound impact on the company's manufacturing processes and quality control standards. As a compact car designed to compete in a rapidly evolving market, the Nova demanded new approaches to production that would ultimately benefit Chevrolet's entire range of vehicles.

One of the most significant contributions of the Nova program was the streamlining of production processes. The need to produce a high-quality compact car efficiently led Chevrolet to reevaluate its manufacturing techniques. Assembly lines were reconfigured to accommodate the Nova's unique design, with a focus on reducing waste and improving efficiency. This optimization didn't just benefit the Nova; the lessons learned were quickly applied to other Chevrolet models, resulting in faster production times and reduced costs across the board.

The Nova also spurred the implementation of new quality control measures. As a car aimed at budget-conscious consumers, the Nova needed to deliver reliable performance and durability. To meet these demands, Chevrolet introduced more rigorous inspection protocols at various stages of the production process. These included enhanced pre-assembly parts inspections, more frequent quality checks during assembly, and comprehensive final inspections before vehicles were released from the factory. These improved quality control measures soon became standard practice for all Chevrolet models, significantly enhancing the brand's reputation for reliability.

The development of the Nova also led to improvements in Chevrolet's supplier relationships and parts sourcing strategies. The need for high-quality, cost-effective components for the Nova encouraged Chevrolet to forge closer partnerships with its suppliers. This collaborative approach resulted in better communication, more innovative solutions, and ultimately, higher quality parts at competitive prices. The success of this strategy with the Nova led Chevrolet to adopt similar approaches across its entire supply chain, benefiting all of its vehicle lines.

Perhaps most importantly, the lessons learned from the Nova's production were applied to other Chevrolet models. The efficiencies gained, the quality control improvements, and the enhanced supplier relationships all became part of Chevrolet's standard operating procedures. This transfer of knowledge and best practices helped to elevate the quality and competitiveness of Chevrolet's entire product range.

The long-term impact of the Nova on Chevrolet's manufacturing philosophy cannot be overstated. The focus on efficiency, quality, and continuous improvement honed during Nova's production became deeply ingrained in Chevrolet's corporate culture. This shift in mindset helped Chevrolet to remain competitive in an increasingly challenging automotive market, allowing the brand to adapt more quickly to changing consumer demands and technological advancements.

Moreover, the Nova's influence extended beyond just manufacturing processes. It also impacted how Chevrolet approached product development and lifecycle management. The success of the Nova demonstrated the importance of flexibility in design and production, allowing for quick updates and improvements in response to market feedback. This agile approach became a hallmark of Chevrolet's product strategy, enabling the brand to stay ahead of trends and maintain its relevance in a fast-changing industry.

In essence, the Nova catalyzed modernization and improvement across Chevrolet's entire manufacturing operation. Its influence went far beyond the assembly line, reshaping the company's approach to quality, efficiency, and innovation. The manufacturing lessons learned from the Nova helped to position Chevrolet as a leader in automotive production, setting new standards that would benefit the brand for decades to come. As such, the Nova's impact on Chevrolet's manufacturing and quality control stands as one of its most significant and enduring legacies.

Section 5.6: Nova's Contribution to Chevrolet's International Presence

The Chevrolet Nova, while primarily designed for the American market, played a significant role in shaping Chevrolet's international presence. As the automotive industry became increasingly globalized in the 1960s and 1970s, the Nova became an ambassador for the Chevrolet brand in various global markets.

Exporting the Nova to international markets was a strategic move for Chevrolet. The compact car's blend of American styling and practicality made it an attractive option for consumers in countries where larger American vehicles were often seen as too big or fuel-inefficient. In markets such as Canada, Mexico, and parts of South America, the Nova found a receptive audience. For instance, in Venezuela, the Nova was marketed as the Chevrolet Chevy II and became a popular choice among middle-class families and young professionals.

Adapting the Nova for different global preferences was a crucial learning experience for Chevrolet. In some markets, the company had to make adjustments to comply with local regulations or meet consumer expectations. For example, in certain European countries,

Chevrolet offered the Nova with smaller, more fuel-efficient engines to align with local preferences and fuel costs. These adaptations taught Chevrolet valuable lessons about the importance of market-specific customization, a principle that would become increasingly important in the company's future global strategies.

The Nova's presence in foreign markets played a significant role in building Chevrolet's reputation internationally. In many countries, the Nova was one of the first Chevrolet models to gain widespread recognition. Its reliability, affordability, and American flair helped create positive associations with the Chevrolet brand. This goodwill paved the way for the introduction of other Chevrolet models in these markets, establishing a foothold for the brand in key international territories.

The lessons learned from the Nova's international journey were invaluable for Chevrolet's future global endeavors. The company gained insights into the complexities of international marketing, distribution, and after-sales service. They learned about the importance of understanding local automotive cultures and preferences, and how to balance maintaining a consistent brand identity while catering to diverse markets. These lessons would prove crucial as Chevrolet expanded its global presence in the following decades.

Perhaps most importantly, the Nova's influence on Chevrolet's global strategy was profound and long-lasting. The success of the Nova in select international markets encouraged Chevrolet to adopt a more global approach to its product planning and marketing strategies. It sparked discussions within the company about developing truly global vehicles that could be sold with minimal modifications across multiple markets. This shift in thinking would eventually lead to more internationally-focused models and a more cohesive global brand strategy for Chevrolet.

The Nova's international presence also helped Chevrolet establish meaningful partnerships and distribution networks in foreign markets. These relationships would prove invaluable as the company continued to expand its global footprint in the years to come. In many ways, the Nova served as a trailblazer, opening doors for Chevrolet in markets where American cars had previously struggled to gain traction.

In conclusion, while the Nova may not have been Chevrolet's first or most successful international model, its contribution to the brand's global presence was significant. It helped Chevrolet learn crucial lessons about international markets, adapt its products for diverse consumer preferences, and build its reputation beyond American shores. The Nova's international journey laid the necessary groundwork for Chevrolet's future as a truly global automotive brand.

Section 5.7: The Nova's Legacy in Chevrolet's Product Development

The Chevy II Nova's influence on Chevrolet extended far beyond its production years, leaving an indelible mark on the brand's approach to product development. This compact car became a crucible for innovation, introducing several features and technologies that would later become staples across Chevrolet's lineup.

One of the most significant innovations first introduced in the Nova was the Super Sport (SS) package. This performance-oriented option set a new standard for factory-built high-performance vehicles and paved the way for future SS models across Chevrolet's range. The success of the Nova SS demonstrated the market's appetite for affordable performance cars, influencing the development of iconic models like the Camaro and the Chevelle SS.

The Nova's impact on future Chevrolet models was profound. Its compact yet versatile platform served as a template for subsequent vehicle designs, showcasing how a single chassis could be adapted to meet diverse consumer needs. This flexibility in design became a hallmark of Chevrolet's approach to product development, allowing the brand to respond quickly to changing market demands.

One of the most lasting impacts of the Nova was on Chevrolet's approach to market research. The Nova's success in attracting younger buyers and performance enthusiasts taught Chevrolet valuable lessons about demographics and market segmentation. This experience led to more targeted research methods and a deeper understanding of diverse consumer preferences, which continue to inform Chevrolet's product strategy to this day.

The Nova also played a crucial role in shaping Chevrolet's product lifecycle management. The car's evolution over its multiple generations demonstrated the importance of continuous improvement and adaptation. Chevrolet learned to strike a balance between retaining popular features and introducing new technologies and design elements. This strategy has become central to the brand's approach to model updates and redesigns.

Lastly, the Nova's enduring influence on Chevrolet's brand values cannot be overstated. The car embodied the principles of affordability, reliability, and performance that have become synonymous with the Chevrolet name. It showed that a well-designed, versatile vehicle could appeal to a broad spectrum of consumers without compromising on quality or excitement.

The lessons learned from the Nova's development and market performance continue to resonate within Chevrolet's halls. From its influence on design philosophy to its impact on marketing strategies, the Nova's legacy lives on in every Chevrolet vehicle that rolls off the production line. It serves as a reminder of the power of innovation, adaptability, and consumer-focused design in building a successful automotive brand.

Chevy II Nova: Power, Passion, and Performance

In many ways, the Chevy II Nova was more than just a car; it was a catalyst for change within Chevrolet. Its success challenged the brand to think differently about its products, its consumers, and its place in the automotive market. As Chevrolet continues to evolve and face new challenges in the 21st century, the spirit of innovation and adaptability exemplified by the Nova remains a guiding light, ensuring that the brand stays true to its roots while pushing the boundaries of automotive excellence.

Chapter 6: The Golden Age: Nova's Role in the Muscle Car Era

Section 6.1: Setting the Stage: The Birth of the Muscle Car Era

The 1960s ushered in a revolutionary period in American automotive history, known as the muscle car era. The golden age of high-performance vehicles transformed the American road landscape and left an indelible mark on car culture. To truly appreciate the Nova's role in this pivotal time, we must first understand the context that gave birth to these powerful machines.

The muscle car era is defined by its emphasis on raw power and straight-line speed. These vehicles typically featured large-displacement V8 engines crammed into midsize car bodies, creating a potent combination of power and relative affordability. The result was a class of cars that could tear up drag strips on weekends and serve as daily drivers during the week, appealing to a wide range of enthusiasts.

Several social and cultural factors fueled the muscle car craze. The post-World War II economic boom had created a prosperous middle class with disposable income and a taste for excitement. The baby boomer generation was coming of age, bringing with them a youth-oriented culture that valued freedom, rebellion, and self-expression. Cars became more than just transportation; they were extensions of personal identity and status symbols.

At the dawn of the muscle car era, the automotive landscape was dominated by large, comfortable cruisers. However, a shift was occurring as manufacturers began to recognize the growing demand for performance-oriented vehicles. Pontiac's 1964 GTO is often credited with kickstarting the muscle car trend, though seeds had been planted earlier with vehicles like the Chrysler 300 and the Chevrolet Impala SS.

As the muscle car market began to take shape, key players emerged. Ford's Mustang, while technically a pony car, helped pave the way for the performance-oriented mindset. Pontiac's GTO, Oldsmobile's 442, and Plymouth's Road Runner quickly became formidable contenders. Dodge entered the fray with the Charger and Challenger, while AMC, though smaller, made its presence known with the AMX and Javelin.

Chevrolet, already a powerhouse in the automotive world, recognized the potential of this growing market. The brand's strategy was multi-faceted, leveraging its existing models while developing new offerings to compete across various segments. The Corvette continued to serve as the brand's halo car, while the Camaro was introduced in 1967 as a direct competitor to the Mustang.

In this competitive landscape, Chevrolet saw an opportunity to transform its compact Chevy II Nova into a genuine muscle car contender. The Nova's journey from an economical family car to a fire-breathing performance machine was about to begin, setting the stage for its significant role in the muscle car era.

As we delve deeper into the Nova's evolution, we'll explore how Chevrolet's engineers and designers rose to the challenge, creating a vehicle that would not only hold its own against the competition but also carve out a unique place in muscle car history. The stage was set, and the Nova was poised to make its mark in the new era of American automotive performance.

Section 6.2: The Nova's Transformation: From Compact to Muscle

The Chevrolet Nova's journey from a modest compact car to a formidable muscle car contender is a testament to the evolving automotive landscape of the 1960s. This transformation wasn't just about increased horsepower; it was a complete reimagining of the Nova's identity and purpose.

When the Chevy II Nova first hit the streets in 1962, it was designed as an economical, no-frills compact car. Its initial purpose was to compete with Ford's popular Falcon, offering American families an affordable and practical transportation option. However, as the muscle car craze began to take hold, Chevrolet recognized the potential to evolve the Nova into something more exciting and performance-oriented.

The Nova's metamorphosis began with subtle yet significant design changes. The once conservative styling gave way to more aggressive lines and a bolder presence. The front grille became more pronounced, the body lines more sculpted, and the overall stance more athletic. These aesthetic modifications weren't just for show; they signaled a shift in the Nova's purpose and appeal.

The most crucial aspect of the Nova's transformation was the introduction of more powerful engine options. While early Novas were equipped with modest inline-four and six-cylinder engines, Chevrolet began offering V8 powerplants that dramatically increased the car's performance capabilities. The 1964 model year marked a significant milestone when the 195-horsepower, 283-cubic-inch V8 became available, giving the Nova the muscle to match its increasingly sporty appearance.

As the muscle car era hit its stride, Chevrolet continued to push the envelope with the Nova. The introduction of the SS (Super Sport) package in 1963 was a game-changer, offering performance-minded buyers a factory-built hot rod. The SS package initially included special trim and badges, but it quickly evolved to encompass more substantial performance upgrades.

By 1966, the Nova SS could be equipped with the mighty 327-cubic-inch V8, producing up to 350 horsepower. This powerplant transformed the once-humble Nova into a legitimate street brawler, capable of holding its own against purpose-built muscle cars from other manufacturers.

The Nova's interior also received attention during this transformation. Sport bucket seats, floor-mounted shifters, and performance-oriented gauges became available, enhancing the driving experience and appealing to enthusiasts who wanted more than just straight-line speed.

Consumer reception to the Nova's muscle car transformation was overwhelmingly positive. Young buyers, in particular, were drawn to the Nova's combination of compact size, aggressive styling, and potent performance. The Nova offered an attractive alternative to larger, more expensive muscle cars, making high-performance motoring accessible to a broader range of enthusiasts.

Sales figures reflected this enthusiasm. As more performance-oriented options became available, Nova sales climbed. The SS models, in particular, saw strong demand, with buyers willing to pay a premium for the added performance and prestige.

The Nova's evolution from compact to muscle car wasn't without challenges. Chevrolet had to carefully balance performance improvements with the need to maintain the Nova's affordability and practicality. Additionally, as a smaller platform, engineers had to work diligently to ensure the Nova could handle the increased power output safely and effectively.

By the late 1960s, the Nova had completed its transformation. No longer just an economy car, it had become a respected member of the muscle car fraternity. The Nova proved that high performance wasn't limited to large, expensive vehicles, democratizing the muscle car experience for a new generation of enthusiasts.

The Nova's journey from compact to muscle car is more than just a story of increased horsepower and aggressive styling. It represents the adaptability of American car culture, the ingenuity of automotive engineers, and the changing tastes of consumers during one of the most exciting eras in automotive history. The Nova's transformation cemented its place in muscle car lore and set the stage for its continued evolution in the years to come.

Section 6.3: Nova SS: The Super Sport Sensation

The Nova SS stands as a shining testament to Chevrolet's commitment to performance during the muscle car era. Introduced in 1963, the Super Sport package transformed the modest Nova into a formidable contender in the high-performance arena. The SS badge, already synonymous with power and prestige on other Chevrolet models, brought a new level of excitement to the Nova lineup.

At the heart of the Nova SS was its powerful engine options. While early models offered a respectable 194 cubic inch inline-six, it was the introduction of V8 engines that truly set the Nova SS apart. The 283 cubic inch V8, capable of producing up to 220 horsepower, gave the Nova SS the muscle to compete with larger, more established performance cars. As the years progressed, even more potent engines became available, including the legendary 350 cubic inch V8 and the monstrous 396 cubic inch big-block V8, which could churn out an impressive 375 horsepower.

Chevy II Nova: Power, Passion, and Performance

The Nova SS wasn't just about raw power; it was a complete performance package. Upgraded suspension components, including heavy-duty springs and shocks, improved handling and cornering abilities. Larger brakes were added to rein in the increased horsepower, while a floor-mounted shifter (either for the manual or automatic transmission) provided drivers with a more engaging driving experience. Visually, the SS package set itself apart with unique badging, special wheel covers or rally wheels, and often, bold racing stripes that left no doubt about the car's performance pedigree.

When compared to its muscle car contemporaries, the Nova SS held its own admirably. While it may not have had the sheer size of a Pontiac GTO or the iconic status of a Ford Mustang, the Nova SS offered a compelling blend of performance and practicality. Its smaller size and lighter weight made it more nimble than some of its larger competitors, while its potent engine options ensured it could keep pace on the drag strip. The Nova SS also had a price advantage, often coming in cheaper than its rivals, making high-performance accessible to a broader range of enthusiasts.

Throughout its run, Chevrolet introduced several notable Nova SS variants and special editions that further cemented its place in muscle car lore. The 1968 Nova SS 396 was a particular highlight, combining the compact Nova body with Chevrolet's powerful big-block engine. The Yenko Novas, while not official factory products, were dealer-modified Novas that pushed performance to the extreme, often equipped with the Corvette's 427 cubic inch engine. These rare and powerful machines have become some of the most sought-after collector cars from the era.

The impact of the Nova SS on Chevrolet's performance reputation cannot be overstated. It proved that the bowtie brand could deliver exhilarating performance in a compact package, expanding the appeal of muscle cars beyond the traditional full-size offerings. The Nova SS helped Chevrolet appeal to a younger demographic, those who wanted the thrill of a high-performance vehicle without the bulk or cost of larger models.

Moreover, the Nova SS served as a testbed for performance technologies that would later be incorporated into other Chevrolet models. Its success paved the way for future compact performance cars and influenced Chevrolet's performance philosophy for years to come. The Nova SS showed that performance wasn't just about big cars with big engines; it was about achieving the perfect balance of power, handling, and everyday usability.

As the muscle car era progressed, the Nova SS continued to evolve, always staying competitive in an increasingly crowded field. Its combination of affordability, performance, and style made it a favorite among enthusiasts and helped establish a loyal following that persists to this day. The Nova SS wasn't just a participant in the muscle car era; it was a defining player, embodying the spirit of accessible performance that characterized this golden age of American automobiles.

Section 6.4: Nova on the Strip: Racing Heritage

The Chevrolet Nova's presence on the drag racing circuit during the muscle car era was nothing short of spectacular. As the compact car transformed into a formidable performance machine, it quickly found its way onto drag strips across America, cementing its place in racing history.

Nova's lightweight chassis and potent engine options made it a natural fit for drag racing. Enthusiasts and professional racers alike recognized the potential of this unassuming Chevrolet, and soon, Novas were lining up at the Christmas tree lights, ready to roar down the quarter-mile.

One of the most notable racing victories for the Nova came in 1968 when Bill "Grumpy" Jenkins piloted his 1968 Nova SS to victory in the NHRA Winternationals. Jenkins' Nova, affectionately known as the "Grumpy's Toy V," dominated the Super Stock class and set numerous records. This victory not only showcased the Nova's capabilities but also inspired countless other racers to choose the Nova as their weapon of choice on the strip.

Chevrolet, recognizing the marketing potential of racing success, threw its support behind several Nova racing initiatives. The company provided factory support to select teams, offering them the latest performance parts and engineering expertise. This symbiotic relationship between Chevrolet and the racing community led to rapid advancements in Nova's performance capabilities, with innovations often making their way from the track to production models.

The Nova's success on the drag strip had a profound impact on its street credibility. As news of racing victories spread, the Nova's reputation as a serious performance car grew. Young enthusiasts, eager to emulate their racing heroes, flocked to Chevrolet dealerships to purchase their own Novas. The phrase "Win on Sunday, sell on Monday" certainly rang true for the Nova during this era.

Racing success also played a crucial role in the Nova's design and engineering evolution. The demands of competitive racing prompted Chevrolet engineers to improve the Nova's performance continually. Lessons learned on the track led to advancements in engine technology, suspension tuning, and aerodynamics. These improvements not only benefited racers but also found their way into production Novas, enhancing the performance of street cars.

One of the most significant racing-inspired innovations was the introduction of the COPO (Central Office Production Order) Nova. These special-order vehicles, often built for racing purposes, featured high-performance engines and specialized equipment not available on regular production models. The COPO Novas became legends in their own right, further solidifying the Nova's racing pedigree.

The Nova's racing heritage extended beyond the quarter-mile as well. Modified Novas also found success in other forms of motorsport, including road racing and even off-road competitions. This versatility demonstrated the Nova's robust design and adaptability, qualities that endeared it to a wide range of automotive enthusiasts.

As the 1960s gave way to the 1970s, the Nova continued to be a force on the drag strip. Even as emissions regulations began to tighten and the muscle car era waned, racers continued to extract impressive performance from their Novas. The platform's potential for modification and its proven track record ensured its continued presence in grassroots racing long after production of the original muscle car era Novas had ceased.

Today, the Nova's racing heritage is celebrated at car shows, nostalgia drag racing events, and in the garages of enthusiasts worldwide. Restored and modified Novas still grace drag strips, carrying on the legacy of their forebears. The thunderous roar of a race-prepared Nova engine serves as a visceral reminder of an era when this unassuming Chevrolet compact car became a giant-killer on America's drag strips.

The Nova's racing heritage is more than just a collection of trophies and elapsed times. It represents a pivotal chapter in the car's history, one that transformed its image, drove its development, and secured its place in the pantheon of American performance cars. The lessons learned and the reputation earned on the strip continue to influence the Nova's legacy, ensuring that this compact Chevrolet will always be remembered as a true racing icon of the muscle car era.

Section 6.5: Nova in Popular Culture: The Muscle Car Icon

The Chevrolet Nova's impact during the muscle car era extended far beyond the realm of automotive engineering and performance. It firmly established itself as a cultural icon, leaving an indelible mark on popular media and becoming a symbol of an entire generation's aspirations and rebellious spirit.

In the world of cinema and television, the Nova became a familiar sight, often cast as the vehicle of choice for characters embodying youth, independence, and a hint of rebellion. Its sleek lines and powerful presence made it a natural fit for high-octane chase scenes and dramatic entrances. Notable appearances included the 1971 film "Two-Lane Blacktop," where a stripped-down 1955 Chevy (often mistaken for a Nova) starred alongside James Taylor and Dennis Wilson. The Nova also made memorable cameos in TV shows like "The Mod Squad" and "Adam-12," further cementing its place in the collective consciousness of American viewers.

The music industry, too, embraced the Nova as a symbol of freedom and power. Rock and roll artists of the era often referenced muscle cars in their lyrics, with the Nova making appearances in songs that captured the spirit of the times. The car's association with speed and rebellion made it a perfect metaphor for the fast-paced, rule-breaking ethos of rock music.

Automotive literature and magazines of the period frequently featured the Nova, particularly the high-performance SS models. Car enthusiasts eagerly devoured articles detailing the latest Nova models, performance upgrades, and racing successes. The Nova's presence in these publications not only boosted its reputation among gearheads but also helped to educate a wider audience about its capabilities and appeal.

As the Nova evolved into an actual muscle car, it became a potent symbol of youth culture and rebellion. Young people saw in the Nova a vehicle that could express their desire for independence and their rejection of the status quo. The car's relatively affordable price point, compared to some other muscle cars, made it an attainable dream for many young enthusiasts, further enhancing its appeal and cultural significance.

Chevy II Nova: Power, Passion, and Performance

Chevrolet's marketing department recognized the Nova's growing cultural cache and crafted advertising campaigns that tapped into this zeitgeist. Advertisements from the era often portrayed the Nova in settings that emphasized youth, freedom, and adventure. Slogans like "Nova: The Great American Value" and "Nova SS: The Lightweight Heavyweight" cleverly positioned the car as both accessible and formidable. These marketing efforts not only boosted sales but also reinforced the Nova's place in popular culture.

The Nova also attracted several notable owners and enthusiasts during this period. From Hollywood celebrities to professional athletes, many public figures chose the Nova as their ride of choice. These high-profile owners further elevated the Nova's status and helped to solidify its reputation as a desirable and superb vehicle.

Car clubs dedicated to the Nova began to spring up across the country, providing a community for enthusiasts to share their passion. These clubs organized meetups, races, and restoration projects, fostering a sense of camaraderie among Nova owners and keeping the car's legacy alive.

The Nova's cultural impact during the muscle car era was profound and lasting. It transcended its role as a mere mode of transportation to become a symbol of an entire generation's hopes, dreams, and rebellious spirit. The car's presence in film, television, music, and literature ensured that it would be remembered not just for its performance on the road but for its place in the hearts and minds of the American public. This cultural resonance would continue to influence perceptions of the Nova long after the muscle car era had passed, cementing its status as a true automotive icon.

Section 6.6: Engineering Innovations: Nova's Technological Advancements

The muscle car era wasn't just about raw power; it was also a time of significant technological advancement in the automotive industry. The Chevy Nova, in its quest to stay competitive and relevant, embraced this spirit of innovation, introducing several engineering improvements that set it apart from its predecessors and rivals.

One of the most significant engineering improvements during this period was the introduction of the high-performance small-block V8 engines. Chevrolet's engineers worked tirelessly to squeeze more power out of smaller, more efficient engines. The result was a range of potent powerplants that could propel the Nova from 0-60 mph in times that were previously unthinkable for a compact car. These engines weren't just about straight-line speed; they were marvels of engineering that balanced power, reliability, and (for the time) fuel efficiency.

The Nova also saw advancements in its suspension system during the muscle car era. Engineers recognized that with great power comes the need for excellent control, and they set about redesigning the Nova's suspension to handle the increased performance. This led to the introduction of heavy-duty springs, specially tuned shock absorbers, and reinforced subframes. These improvements not only enhanced the Nova's handling characteristics but also contributed to a more comfortable ride, striking a balance between performance and daily drivability.

Another innovative feature introduced in muscle car-era Novas was the adoption of disc brakes. Initially offered as an option and later becoming standard on high-performance models, disc brakes significantly improved the Nova's stopping power. This was a crucial advancement, given the increased speeds these cars were capable of achieving. The move to disc brakes not only enhanced safety but also improved the overall driving experience, allowing drivers to push their Novas harder with greater confidence.

These advancements in engine technology, suspension design, and braking systems collectively transformed the Nova's performance and handling. The compact car that once prioritized economy and practicality could now hold its own against purpose-built performance machines. The Nova became known for its nimble handling, a characteristic that set it apart from some of its larger, heavier muscle car competitors.

When compared to its contemporaries, the Nova's technological offerings were impressive. While some competitors focused solely on straight-line speed, the Nova offered a more well-rounded package. Its combination of powerful engines, improved handling, and enhanced braking made it a versatile performer both on the street and the strip. This holistic approach to performance engineering helped the Nova carve out its unique niche in the muscle car market.

The innovations introduced during this era had a lasting impact on future Chevrolet models. The lessons learned from pushing the limits of the Nova's compact platform would inform the development of subsequent Chevrolet vehicles. The advancements in engine technology, particularly in the realm of small-block V8s, would become a cornerstone of Chevrolet's performance offerings for decades to come.

Moreover, the emphasis on balancing performance with practicality that characterized the Nova's development during this period would become a defining trait of Chevrolet's approach to building performance cars. This philosophy of creating vehicles that could deliver exhilarating performance without sacrificing everyday usability would influence everything from future Camaros to modern-day performance sedans.

In essence, the engineering innovations of the muscle car era Nova represented more than just improvements to a single model. They were a testament to Chevrolet's commitment to pushing the boundaries of automotive technology. This commitment would continue to drive the brand forward long after the golden age of muscle cars had passed.

Section 6.7: The Legacy of Muscle Car Era Novas

The impact of the Chevy Nova during the muscle car era reverberates through automotive history, leaving an indelible mark on car culture and the Chevrolet brand. This legacy is multifaceted, touching on aspects of collectibility, design influence, brand identity, and the Nova's place in the pantheon of muscle car legends.

The muscle car era Novas have become highly sought-after collector's items, with pristine examples commanding impressive prices at auctions and private sales. The Nova SS models, in particular, are prized possessions for enthusiasts and collectors alike. Their rarity, combined with their historical significance, has elevated these vehicles to the status of automotive treasures. The value of these classic Novas continues to appreciate, reflecting not just their scarcity but also the enduring appeal of the muscle car ethos they represent.

The design language and engineering principles developed during the Nova's muscle car years had a lasting influence on future Chevrolet models. The aggressive styling cues, performance-oriented features, and powerful engine options that defined the muscle car era, the Novas set a template that Chevrolet would draw upon for decades to come. This influence can be seen in subsequent Nova generations and even in modern Chevrolet performance vehicles, which often pay homage to their muscle car ancestors in both design and spirit.

One of the most significant aspects of the muscle car era Nova's legacy is its role in shaping Chevrolet's brand identity. During this period, the Nova transformed from a modest compact car to a formidable performance machine, mirroring Chevrolet's own evolution as a brand. The success and popularity of the muscle car Novas helped cement Chevrolet's reputation as a manufacturer of exciting, powerful, and attainable performance vehicles. This association with performance and excitement remains a core part of Chevrolet's brand identity to this day.

In the broader context of muscle car history, the Nova holds a special place. While it may not have been the first or the most powerful muscle car, its accessibility and versatility made it a unique player in the muscle car scene. The Nova demonstrated that high performance wasn't limited to large, expensive vehicles, bringing the thrill of muscle car ownership to a broader audience. This democratization of performance helped spread the muscle car culture and contributed to its enduring popularity.

The legacy of the muscle car era Novas extends beyond the realm of automotive enthusiasts. These vehicles have become cultural icons, representing an era of American optimism, innovation, and unbridled automotive passion. They appear in movies, television shows, and music videos, serving as shorthand for a particular time and place in American history. The muscle car Nova has become a symbol of freedom, youth, and rebellion; its image is instantly recognizable, even to those who may not be car enthusiasts.

Today, the muscle car era Novas continue to inspire and excite. Restoration projects bring these classics back to their former glory, while custom builds pay homage to the Nova's performance legacy with modern twists. Car shows and cruise nights across the country feature proud Nova owners showcasing their meticulously maintained or lovingly restored vehicles, keeping the spirit of the muscle car era alive.

The Nova's journey through the muscle car era was more than just a chapter in the model's history; it was a transformative period that defined the car's identity and secured its place in automotive lore. From its humble beginnings as a compact car to its evolution into a bona fide muscle machine, the Nova's story is one of adaptation, innovation, and the pursuit of performance. As we look back on this golden age of American automobiles, the Chevy Nova stands as a testament to the ingenuity, passion, and sheer excitement that defined the muscle car era.

Chapter 7: Innovations and Advancements: Nova's Technological Leaps

Section 7.1: Engine Innovations

The heart of any great car lies beneath its hood, and the Chevy II Nova was no exception. Throughout its production run, the Nova saw a series of groundbreaking engine innovations that not only set it apart from its competitors but also paved the way for future advancements in automotive engineering.

The most significant leap forward came with the introduction of the Small-Block V8 engine. This compact yet powerful engine would become a game-changer for the Nova, transforming it from a modest family car into a formidable muscle car contender. The Small-Block V8's lightweight design and impressive power output allowed the Nova to achieve a remarkable power-to-weight ratio, setting new standards for performance in its class.

As the Nova evolved, so did its engine options. Chevrolet continuously refined and expanded the range of available powerplants, catering to a diverse array of drivers, from those seeking economical daily transportation to enthusiasts craving raw, unbridled power. This evolution saw the introduction of increasingly potent V8 variants, as well as more efficient inline-six options, ensuring that there was a Nova engine configuration to suit every need and desire.

Performance enhancements and tuning capabilities became a hallmark of the Nova's engine lineup. Chevrolet engineers worked tirelessly to squeeze every ounce of power from these motors, implementing advanced camshaft profiles, high-flow cylinder heads, and optimized intake and exhaust systems. These improvements not only boosted horsepower and torque figures but also enhanced the Nova's responsiveness and driving dynamics.

The Nova was also at the forefront of fuel injection advancements. As carburetors began to fall out of favor due to their inefficiency and high maintenance requirements, Chevrolet started introducing fuel injection systems to the Nova. This transition brought about improved fuel economy, more precise engine management, and enhanced cold-start reliability. The move to fuel injection represented a significant leap forward in engine technology, setting the stage for the sophisticated electronic fuel injection systems we see in modern vehicles.

Amidst the pursuit of performance, Chevrolet didn't lose sight of evolving environmental concerns. The Nova played a crucial role in the development and integration of emissions control technology. As regulations tightened, Chevrolet rose to the challenge, implementing catalytic converters, exhaust gas recirculation systems, and other technologies that reduced pollution. These advancements allowed the Nova to maintain its performance edge while meeting increasingly stringent emissions standards.

The engine innovations showcased in the Chevy II Nova weren't just about raw power or efficiency in isolation. They represented a holistic approach to engine design that balanced performance, reliability, and environmental responsibility. This forward-thinking approach would influence Chevrolet's engine development for decades to come, cementing the Nova's place not just in the hearts of enthusiasts but in the annals of automotive engineering history.

Section 7.2: Transmission and Drivetrain Advancements

The Chevrolet Nova's evolution wasn't limited to its iconic engines; significant advancements in transmission and drivetrain technology played a crucial role in its performance and popularity. These improvements enhanced the driving experience, making the Nova more versatile and appealing to a broader range of enthusiasts.

One of the most notable developments was the continuous improvement of manual transmissions. Early Nova models were equipped with three-speed manual transmissions, which were sturdy but limited in terms of both performance and fuel economy. As the Nova progressed, Chevrolet introduced four-speed manual transmissions, offering better gear ratios for improved acceleration and top speed. These transmissions featured synchromesh on all forward gears, ensuring smoother shifts and reduced wear. By the late 1960s, some high-performance Nova models even offered close-ratio four-speed transmissions, further enhancing the car's racing capabilities.

Automatic transmissions also saw significant advancements during the Nova's production run. The introduction of the two-speed Powerglide automatic In early models provided a convenient option for drivers who preferred not to shift gears manually. However, the real breakthrough came with the three-speed Turbo Hydra-Matic transmission. This robust and efficient automatic transmission offered better performance and fuel economy compared to its predecessor. It became a popular option, especially when paired with the Nova's more powerful V8 engines.

Rear axle and differential enhancements were another area of focus for Chevrolet engineers. The Nova saw the introduction of various gear ratios to suit different driving styles and performance needs. Performance-oriented models could be equipped with limited-slip differentials, which improved traction and handling, particularly during acceleration and cornering. These advancements allowed Nova drivers to put more power to the ground effectively.

Driveshaft and U-joint innovations also contributed to the Nova's improved performance and reliability. Stronger materials and better manufacturing techniques resulted in driveshafts that could handle increased power output from the more potent engines. Universal joints (U-joints) saw similar improvements, with more durable designs that could withstand the increased stress of high-performance driving.

As the automotive industry progressed, so did traction control technologies. While early Novas relied solely on mechanical systems and driver skill, later models began to incorporate rudimentary forms of traction control. These systems, though not as sophisticated as modern electronic stability control, helped drivers maintain better control of their vehicles under various driving conditions.

The combined effect of these transmission and drivetrain advancements was a Nova that became increasingly capable and enjoyable to drive. Whether equipped with a manual transmission for maximum driver engagement or an automatic for convenience, the Nova's drivetrain evolved to efficiently transfer power from its increasingly potent engines to the road.

These improvements not only enhanced the Nova's performance credentials but also contributed to its versatility. The car could now seamlessly transition from a comfortable daily driver to a weekend warrior at the drag strip, thanks to its robust and advanced drivetrain components.

Moreover, many of these advancements laid the groundwork for future Chevrolet models. The lessons learned and technologies developed for the Nova's transmission and drivetrain systems would go on to influence the design of other iconic Chevrolet vehicles, cementing the Nova's place as a pivotal model in the brand's history.

In essence, the transmission and drivetrain advancements in the Chevrolet Nova represented a perfect synergy of performance, reliability, and driver comfort. These improvements played a significant role in shaping the Nova's character and contributed substantially to its enduring popularity among automotive enthusiasts.

Section 7.3: Suspension and Handling Upgrades

The Chevy II Nova's journey from a humble compact car to a muscle car icon was not just about raw power; it was equally about how that power was delivered to the road. Throughout its production run, the Nova saw significant advancements in suspension and handling, transforming it into a car that could not only accelerate quickly but also corner and brake with precision.

One of the most notable improvements came in the form of the front suspension design evolution. Early Nova models featured a simple coil spring front suspension, which was adequate for everyday driving but left much to be desired in terms of performance and handling. As the Nova grew more powerful, Chevrolet engineers recognized the need for a more sophisticated setup. They introduced a double A-arm front suspension system, which provided better geometry and allowed for improved camber control during cornering. This change significantly enhanced the Nova's stability and responsiveness, particularly when fitted with larger, more powerful engines.

The rear suspension of the Nova also saw considerable improvements over time. The initial leaf spring design, while robust and cost-effective, was prone to axle hop under hard acceleration, a particular issue for high-performance variants. To address this, Chevrolet implemented multi-leaf springs with staggered shock absorber mounting points. This modification helped to reduce axle hop and improve traction, allowing drivers to put more power to the ground without sacrificing control.

Steering system advancements played a crucial role in enhancing the Nova's handling characteristics. The introduction of power steering as an option in later models made the car more manageable at low speeds without sacrificing road feel at higher velocities. Additionally, the implementation of a quicker steering ratio in performance-oriented models gave drivers more precise control, essential for both spirited street driving and competitive events.

One of the most critical areas of improvement was in the Nova's braking system. As engine power increased, so did the need for more effective stopping power. Early drum brakes gave way to disc brakes, first introduced on the front axle and later made available on all four wheels in select models. This upgrade dramatically reduced brake fade during repeated hard stops and provided more consistent pedal feel. The introduction of power brake boosters further enhanced the Nova's stopping capabilities, giving drivers more confidence to exploit the car's performance potential.

Tire and wheel technology progressed in tandem with the Nova's other handling upgrades. As the car evolved, it saw the introduction of wider wheels and tires, providing a larger contact patch with the road. This improved both traction and cornering stability. The shift from bias-ply to radial tires was another significant advancement, offering better handling characteristics, improved ride quality, and increased longevity.

These suspension and handling upgrades weren't just about improving performance metrics; they fundamentally changed the driving experience of the Nova. The car became more balanced, responsive, and capable of handling its increased power output.

Drivers could now push the Nova harder into corners with confidence, brake later, and accelerate out of turns more aggressively.

Moreover, these advancements weren't limited to high-performance variants. Even base model Novas benefited from the trickle-down effect of these technologies, resulting in a more comfortable and controlled ride for everyday drivers.

The Nova's suspension and handling evolution is a testament to Chevrolet's commitment to continuous improvement. Each upgrade was a response to the changing needs and expectations of drivers, as well as advancements in automotive technology. These improvements not only enhanced the Nova's performance credentials but also contributed to its versatility as a comfortable daily driver and a weekend warrior.

By the end of its production run, the Chevy II Nova had transformed from a modest compact into a well-rounded performance machine, capable of holding its own against purpose-built sports cars of the era. The lessons learned and technologies developed during the Nova's evolution would go on to influence future Chevrolet models, cementing its place not just in the hearts of enthusiasts but in the annals of automotive engineering history.

Section 7.4: Body and Chassis Developments

The Chevy II Nova's body and chassis underwent significant developments throughout its production run, showcasing Chevrolet's commitment to innovation and improvement. These advancements not only enhanced the vehicle's performance and durability but also contributed to its iconic status in automotive history.

One of the most notable advancements in the Nova's body construction was the introduction of unibody architecture. This revolutionary design integrated the body and frame into a single structure, replacing the traditional body-on-frame construction. The unibody design offered several advantages, including increased structural rigidity, improved handling, and enhanced crash protection. It also allowed for a lighter overall vehicle weight, which translated to better fuel efficiency and performance.

Weight reduction techniques were a constant focus for Chevrolet engineers working on the Nova. As performance demands increased, so did the need to offset the weight of larger engines and additional features. The use of high-strength, low-alloy (HSLA) steel in strategic areas of the body allowed for thinner panels without compromising structural integrity. Additionally, the incorporation of aluminum components in non-structural areas further contributed to weight savings.

Aerodynamic improvements played a crucial role in the Nova's evolution, particularly in its later years. While early models featured a boxy, utilitarian design, later generations saw more streamlined profiles. The front grille and bumper designs were refined to reduce air resistance, while the overall body shape became more wind-cheating. These aerodynamic enhancements not only improved fuel efficiency but also contributed to better high-speed stability and reduced wind noise.

Rust prevention and corrosion resistance were significant concerns for automakers during the Nova's era, and Chevrolet made substantial strides in addressing these issues. The introduction of galvanized steel panels in critical areas prone to rust, such as rocker panels and wheel wells, significantly improved the Nova's longevity. Additionally, improved painting processes and the use of rust-inhibiting primers helped protect the body from the elements, addressing a common complaint of earlier models.

Safety feature integrations became increasingly important throughout the Nova's production run, reflecting changing regulations and consumer expectations. The body structure was reinforced to create designated crumple zones, which absorbed impact energy in the event of a collision. Side-impact protection beams were added to the doors, providing additional occupant safety. The integration of a collapsible steering column reduced the risk of driver injury in frontal impacts.

As safety standards evolved, so did the Nova's design. Later models featured improved bumper systems that could absorb low-speed impacts without damage, protecting both the vehicle and its occupants. The implementation of laminated windshields and tempered side glass reduced the risk of injury from shattered glass in accidents.

The evolution of the Nova's body and chassis developments also had a significant impact on its aesthetics. The cleaner lines and more integrated design elements that resulted from these advancements contributed to the car's timeless appeal. The Nova's ability to balance form and function, incorporating cutting-edge technology while maintaining its distinctive look, was a testament to Chevrolet's engineering prowess.

These body and chassis developments not only improved the Nova's performance, safety, and durability but also set new standards for the industry. Many of the advancements pioneered or refined in the Nova would go on to influence future Chevrolet models and the broader automotive landscape.

The Nova's body and chassis developments stand as a testament to Chevrolet's commitment to continuous improvement and innovation. From unibody construction to advanced safety features, these advancements played a crucial role in shaping the Nova's legacy as a versatile, durable, and beloved American automobile.

Section 7.5: Interior and Comfort Innovations

The Chevy II Nova's evolution wasn't limited to its performance capabilities; it also made significant strides in interior comfort and convenience features. As the model progressed through its production years, Chevrolet engineers and designers focused on creating a more luxurious and user-friendly cabin environment.

One of the most noticeable improvements was the evolution of the dashboard and instrument cluster. Early Nova models featured a simple, functional layout with basic gauges and controls. However, as consumer expectations grew, so did the sophistication of the Nova's dashboard. Later models boasted more comprehensive instrument panels, including tachometers, temperature gauges, and even early forms of trip computers. The layout became more driver-centric, with controls placed within easy reach, enhancing both safety and convenience.

Seating comfort and ergonomics saw substantial improvements throughout the Nova's lifespan. The early bench seats, while spacious, lacked the support and adjustability of later designs. As the Nova matured, it introduced bucket seats with improved contours and padding, offering better lateral support for spirited driving. Adjustable headrests became standard, not just for comfort but as a critical safety feature. The introduction of power seat adjustments in higher-end models further enhanced the driving experience, allowing for precise positioning to suit individual preferences.

Climate control advancements were another area where the Nova made significant strides. The rudimentary heating systems of early models gave way to more sophisticated climate control options. Air conditioning, once a luxury option, became more common and efficient in later Nova models. The introduction of multi-speed blowers and adjustable vents enabled better air distribution throughout the cabin, ensuring a comfortable environment for all occupants, regardless of outside temperatures.

Audio system upgrades paralleled the broader technological advancements of the era. The basic AM radios of early Novas evolved into more advanced AM/FM units, with higher-end models eventually offering 8-track and cassette players. Sound quality improved dramatically with the introduction of better speakers and amplifiers. By the end of its production run, some Nova models even featured early forms of digital audio technology, laying the groundwork for the advanced infotainment systems found in modern vehicles.

Interior materials and finish enhancements played a crucial role in elevating the Nova's perceived quality and comfort. Early models featured durable but basic materials, primarily focused on functionality. As the Nova moved upmarket, it began to incorporate more premium materials. Soft-touch plastics replaced hard surfaces, while higher-grade fabrics and optional leather upholstery added a touch of luxury. Attention to detail increased, with better fit and finish, reduced panel gaps, and improved sound insulation contributing to a more refined interior ambiance.

These interior and comfort innovations weren't just about luxury; they represented Chevrolet's response to changing consumer expectations and increasing competition in the market. By continuously improving the Nova's interior, Chevrolet ensured that the model remained competitive and appealing to a broad range of customers, from performance enthusiasts to families seeking a comfortable daily driver.

The evolution of the Nova's interior comfort features also foreshadowed many of the amenities we now take for granted in modern vehicles. The focus on ergonomics, climate control, audio systems, and material quality set a standard that influenced not just future Chevrolet models but the broader automotive industry as a whole.

In essence, the interior and comfort innovations of the Chevy II Nova demonstrated that performance and luxury can coexist without being mutually exclusive. By marrying its powerful engines and capable chassis with an increasingly refined interior, the Nova created a template for the modern performance car that offers excitement on the road without sacrificing comfort and convenience.

Section 7.6: Electrical and Electronic Advancements

The Chevy II Nova's evolution wasn't limited to mechanical improvements; it also saw significant advancements in its electrical and electronic systems. These innovations not only enhanced the car's performance but also improved its reliability, safety, and overall driving experience.

One of the most notable electrical advancements in the Nova was the evolution of its ignition system. Early models relied on traditional points-and-condenser ignition systems, which were prone to wear and required frequent maintenance. However, as technology progressed, the Nova incorporated electronic ignition systems. This upgrade significantly improved engine performance, fuel efficiency, and cold-start reliability. The electronic ignition eliminated the need for frequent tune-ups and ensured more consistent spark delivery, resulting in smoother engine operation across all driving conditions.

Lighting technology in the Nova also saw remarkable improvements over its production years. The introduction of halogen headlights in later models provided brighter, more focused illumination, enhancing nighttime visibility and safety. Additionally, the Nova's interior lighting evolved, with more efficient and durable LED lights gradually replacing traditional incandescent bulbs in various applications.

One of the most significant electronic advancements in the Nova was the introduction of electronic control modules (ECMs). These computer systems revolutionized how the car's engine and other systems functioned. ECMs allowed for more precise control over fuel injection, ignition timing, and emissions, resulting in improved performance, fuel economy, and reduced environmental impact. This technology laid the groundwork for the sophisticated engine management systems found in modern vehicles.

Hand in hand with the introduction of ECMs came advancements in diagnostics and troubleshooting capabilities. The Nova began incorporating on-board diagnostics systems, which could detect and report issues within the vehicle's various electronic systems. This feature not only made it easier for mechanics to identify and resolve problems but also allowed for proactive maintenance, potentially preventing more serious issues down the line.

The Nova's electrical system also saw improvements in its power accessories. As consumer demand for comfort and convenience features grew, the Nova responded with innovations such as power windows, power door locks, and electrically adjustable mirrors. These features, while commonplace today, were significant advancements that enhanced the Nova's appeal and driving experience.

It's worth noting that these electrical and electronic advancements weren't just about adding features or improving performance. They also contributed to the overall reliability and longevity of the Nova. More robust electrical systems meant fewer failures and easier maintenance, factors that undoubtedly contributed to the Nova's enduring popularity.

The electrical and electronic innovations introduced in the Nova throughout its production run were more than just incremental improvements. They represented a shift in automotive technology, moving away from purely mechanical systems towards the electronically controlled vehicles we know today. These advancements not only enhanced the Nova's performance and appeal but also paved the way for future developments in Chevrolet's vehicle lineup and the broader automotive industry.

Section 7.7: Nova's Impact on Future Chevrolet Models

The Chevrolet Nova's influence extends far beyond its own production years, leaving an indelible mark on future Chevrolet models and shaping the company's approach to automotive design and engineering. This section explores the lasting impact of the Nova's innovations and how they continue to resonate in Chevrolet's modern lineup.

Many technologies pioneered or refined in the Nova found their way into later Chevrolet designs. The small-block V8 engine, which became a staple in the Nova, went on to power numerous Chevrolet vehicles, from sports cars to trucks. Its compact design, impressive power output, and reliability made it a favorite among engineers and enthusiasts alike. The lessons learned from tuning and improving this engine in the Nova context directly influenced the development of future Chevrolet powerplants.

The Nova played a crucial role in Chevrolet's development of performance cars. Its combination of a lightweight body and powerful engine options created a formula that Chevrolet would continue to refine in subsequent models. The success of high-performance Nova variants, such as the SS, demonstrated the market potential for affordable, everyday cars with serious performance capabilities. This philosophy would later inform the development of iconic models like the Camaro and the modern-day SS sedan.

Chevrolet applied numerous lessons learned from the Nova to other models in its lineup. The Nova's unibody construction, which provided an excellent balance of rigidity and weight savings, became a blueprint for future Chevrolet vehicles. The company's engineers also applied the knowledge gained from the Nova's suspension tuning to improve the handling characteristics of later models, striking a balance between comfort and sportiness that became a Chevrolet hallmark.

The Nova's influence on modern Chevrolet engineering principles cannot be overstated. The car's development taught Chevrolet valuable lessons about the importance of modularity and scalability in vehicle design. The Nova's platform flexibility, which allowed it to accommodate a wide range of engines and body styles, became a guiding principle in Chevrolet's approach to vehicle architecture. This philosophy of adaptable design continues to inform Chevrolet's strategy, allowing for efficient development of diverse vehicle types on shared platforms.

In today's Chevrolet lineup, the legacy of Nova's innovations lives on. The emphasis on accessible performance, seen in models like the Camaro and Corvette, can be traced back to the Nova's successful formula. The focus on efficient packaging and innovative use of space, evident in modern Chevrolet compact and midsize cars, echoes the Nova's original mission as a compact yet capable vehicle.

Moreover, the Nova's journey from a humble compact to a performance icon has inspired Chevrolet's approach to vehicle evolution. This ethos is reflected in how Chevrolet continually refines and enhances its models, always pushing the boundaries of performance and technology while maintaining a connection to their roots.

The Nova's impact on Chevrolet's engineering culture is its most enduring legacy. The spirit of innovation, the willingness to push boundaries, and the commitment to delivering performance to a broad audience are hallmarks of the Nova program that continue to drive Chevrolet's engineering teams today. As Chevrolet moves into the era of electrification and autonomous vehicles, the lessons learned from the Nova era continue to inform their approach: embracing new technologies, refining them for mass-market appeal, and never losing sight of the driving excitement that has always been at the heart of the Chevrolet brand.

In conclusion, the Chevrolet Nova's technological leaps did more than just define a single model; they helped shape the future of an entire brand. From engine technology to design philosophy, the Nova's DNA can be found throughout Chevrolet's modern lineup, a testament to its enduring influence and the timeless appeal of its innovations.

Chevy II Nova: Power, Passion, and Performance

Chapter 8: Behind the Wheel: Stories from Nova Owners and Drivers

Section 8.1: The First-Time Nova Owner

For many automotive enthusiasts, purchasing their first Chevy II Nova is a momentous occasion, marking the beginning of a passionate journey into the world of classic cars. The thrill of acquiring a Nova is often described as a mix of excitement, nervousness, and sheer joy. One such owner, Mike Thompson from Ohio, recalls the day he bought his 1966 Nova SS: "I had been dreaming about owning a Nova for years, and when I finally found the right one, my hands were shaking as I signed the papers. It was like Christmas morning for a grown-up car enthusiast."

However, the initial excitement of ownership is often followed by a steep learning curve and unexpected challenges. New Nova owners quickly discover that maintaining a classic car requires a distinct set of skills and knowledge compared to modern vehicles. From sourcing period-correct parts to understanding the quirks of carbureted engines, first-time owners find themselves on a crash course in automotive history and mechanics.

Fortunately, the Nova community is known for its welcoming nature and willingness to support newcomers. Online forums, local car clubs, and specialized Nova enthusiast groups provide invaluable resources for first-time owners. These communities offer everything from technical advice to emotional support, helping novice owners navigate the intricacies of Nova ownership. As Sarah Miller, a recent Nova convert, puts it, "I was overwhelmed at first, but the Nova community embraced me. They've been an incredible source of knowledge and encouragement."

The memorable first drives and experiences in a newly acquired Nova often leave lasting impressions on owners. There's something special about hearing the rumble of the engine, feeling the connection to the road through the steering wheel, and experiencing the admiring glances from passersby. John Davis, who bought his first Nova two years ago, shares, "My first real drive in my '68 Nova was a summer evening cruise through the countryside. The sun was setting, the engine was purring, and I felt like I had been transported back in time. It was magical."

Owning a Nova often changes an individual's perception of classic cars. What starts as an interest in a particular model can blossom into a deep appreciation for automotive history and craftsmanship. Many first-time Nova owners find themselves developing a keen eye for detail, learning to spot subtle differences between model years, and gaining a newfound respect for the engineering of yesteryear.

The journey of a first-time Nova owner is one of growth, learning, and passion. It's a path that leads not just to mechanical knowledge and driving enjoyment, but also to a sense of connection with a community and a piece of automotive history. As these owners settle into their role as Nova custodians, they often find that their cars become more than just vehicles – they become cherished companions on a lifelong adventure in classic car enthusiasm.

Section 8.2: The Family Heirloom

The Chevy II Nova has become more than just a car for many families; it's a cherished heirloom passed down through generations. These vehicles carry not only the legacy of automotive history but also the personal histories of the families who have loved and cared for them over the decades.

For many Nova owners, their connection to the car began long before they could even drive. Mark Thompson, a third-generation Nova owner from Ohio, recalls, "My earliest memories are of sitting on my grandfather's lap in his '66 Nova, pretending to steer while it was parked in the driveway. That car was as much a part of our family as any person."

The emotional connections tied to these family Novas run deep. They're not just modes of transportation, but time machines that transport families back to cherished moments. Sarah Rodriguez, whose family has owned their '63 Nova for over 50 years, shares, "Every time I sit in that car, I can almost hear the echoes of laughter from family road trips, or smell my dad's aftershave as he taught me to drive stick."

However, maintaining a family Nova over decades comes with its own set of challenges. As these cars age, finding original parts becomes increasingly complex, and the cost of maintenance can be substantial. Yet, for many families, these challenges are seen as opportunities to bond and create new memories.

"When the transmission in our Nova gave out, my son and I spent every weekend for three months rebuilding it," says Jack Miller, a second-generation Nova owner. "It was frustrating at times, but it taught us both patience and perseverance. Now, every time we drive the car, we feel a sense of shared accomplishment."

Many families have chosen to modify or restore their Novas to keep the legacy alive for future generations. These projects often become family affairs, with different members contributing their skills and learning new ones together. The Patel family of California turned the restoration of their 1967 Nova into a three-generation project, with grandfather, father, and son all working together to bring the car back to its former glory.

"We modernized some aspects for safety and reliability," explains Raj Patel, "but we were careful to maintain the spirit of the original car. It was important to us that future generations could experience the Nova as we did, while also making it practical for today's roads."

Perhaps most touchingly, many families have made their Nova a focal point for reunions and events. The Clark family of Texas has an annual "Nova Day" where all the extended family gathers to admire the car, share stories, and take turns driving it. "It's become our family's unofficial mascot," laughs Linda Clark. "We've even had family photos taken with it at weddings and graduations."

These family heirloom Novas serve as tangible links to the past, connecting generations through a shared love of automotive history. They're not just preserved in garages but in the hearts and memories of the families who cherish them. As Tom Jenkins, whose Nova has been in his family for four generations, puts it, "This car isn't just a piece of metal and engineering. It's a repository of our family's history, a testament to our endurance, and a promise to future generations that some things are worth holding onto."

The story of the family heirloom Nova is one of love, dedication, and the power of shared experiences. It demonstrates that sometimes, the most valuable inheritance isn't measured in dollars, but in the memories and connections forged over years of care and appreciation for a truly special automobile.

Section 8.3: The Restoration Journey

The journey of restoring a Chevy II Nova is a tale of passion, perseverance, and ultimate triumph. For many enthusiasts, the process begins with the thrill of discovery. Picture the scene: a weathered Nova, tucked away in an old barn or forgotten in a distant relative's garage, waiting to be brought back to life. These "barn finds" often spark the imagination of restoration enthusiasts, who see beyond the rust and decay to envision the car's potential glory.

Once a project is acquired, Nova, the real work begins. Restoration is not for the faint of heart; it requires careful planning, extensive research, and often, a significant financial investment. Many restorers speak of the importance of setting realistic goals and timelines. "I thought I could restore my '66 Nova in a year," chuckles Mike Thompson, a Nova enthusiast from Ohio. "Five years later, I'm still at it, but loving every minute."

The process of sourcing parts for a Nova restoration can be both exciting and challenging. While many components are readily available through specialty suppliers, some rare or model-specific parts can prove elusive. Restorers often become detectives, scouring swap meets, online forums, and even junkyards to find that perfect, period-correct piece. The Nova community plays a crucial role here, with enthusiasts often helping each other locate hard-to-find parts or offering advice on suitable alternatives.

Overcoming restoration challenges is a common theme among Nova rebuilders. From dealing with extensive rust repair to deciphering decades-old wiring diagrams, each project presents its unique set of obstacles. "The toughest part of my restoration was getting the engine bay just right," recalls Sarah Martinez, who restored a 1963 Nova SS. "I must have repainted it three times before I was satisfied, but that attention to detail made all the difference in the end."

For many, the most rewarding aspect of Nova restoration is the moment when all the hard work finally pays off. The satisfaction of turning the key and hearing the engine roar to life for the first time in years is often described as indescribable. "When I first drove my restored '68 Nova down the street, I couldn't stop grinning," says Tom Baker, a Nova restorer from California. "All those late nights and skinned knuckles suddenly seemed worth it."

The final stage of many restoration journeys involves showcasing the reborn Nova at car shows and events. This is where restorers can truly see their efforts appreciated by fellow enthusiasts and the general public alike. Many speak of the pride they feel when onlookers marvel at their Nova's gleaming paint and immaculate interior, often not realizing the thousands of hours of work that went into its restoration.

However, for true enthusiasts, the restoration of a Nova is never truly complete. There's always another detail to perfect, another component to upgrade, or another story to share about the process. The restoration journey becomes a part of the car's history, adding depth and personal significance to an already beloved classic.

As Nova restorer Janet Lee puts it, "Restoring my Nova wasn't just about bringing back a car; it was about preserving a piece of automotive history and creating new memories along the way. Every time I look at my Nova now, I see not just a beautiful car, but a reflection of my own dedication and passion."

The restoration journey of a Chevy II Nova is more than just a mechanical process; it's a labor of love that connects enthusiasts to the rich history of this iconic vehicle. It's a testament to the enduring appeal of the Nova and the passionate community that keeps these classics alive and thriving on the roads today.

Section 8.4: The Nova in Competition

The Chevrolet Nova's reputation as a formidable competitor on the racing circuit is well-established, and the stories from drag racing enthusiasts only serve to reinforce this legacy. Many Nova owners have found themselves drawn to the thrill of competition, pushing their beloved cars to the limits on drag strips across the country.

Chevy II Nova: Power, Passion, and Performance

One such enthusiast, Mike Johnson, recalls his first time taking his 1969 Nova SS to the local drag strip. "I had always heard about how well Novas performed in drag racing, but experiencing it firsthand was something else entirely," he says. "The rush of acceleration, the roar of the engine, and the excitement of crossing the finish line. It was addictive from the very first run."

To achieve peak performance, Nova racers often make significant modifications to their vehicles. Standard upgrades include high-performance engines, upgraded transmissions, and enhanced suspension systems. Some racers go as far as to strip their Novas down to the bare essentials, removing unnecessary weight to improve acceleration and speed.

Tom Rodriguez, a veteran Nova racer with over two decades of experience, shares his approach to modifications: "It's all about finding the right balance between power and weight. I've spent years fine-tuning my '66 Nova, constantly tweaking the engine and shaving off ounces wherever I can. Every little adjustment can make a difference when you're racing at this level."

The racing community is filled with tales of memorable races and remarkable achievements. Sarah Chen, who races a 1972 Nova, recounts an inspiring event: "It was the final round of a major regional competition. I was up against a Mustang that had been dominating all day. When the lights turned green, my Nova launched like a rocket. I crossed the finish line first by mere inches, setting a personal best time in the process. The crowd went wild, and that moment solidified my love for Nova racing."

Over the years, the Nova has built a formidable reputation on the racing circuit. Its compact size, combined with the potential for tremendous power, makes it a favorite among drag racers. The car's success has even led to the creation of Nova-specific racing classes at some events, showcasing the model's enduring popularity and competitiveness.

However, for many Nova racers, there's a constant struggle to balance performance upgrades with maintaining the car's authenticity. While some opt for a complete overhaul with modern technology and radical modifications, others prefer to stay true to the Nova's original specifications.

Mark Davis, who races a nearly stock 1967 Nova, explains his philosophy: "For me, it's about proving what these cars were capable of right from the factory. Sure, I might not be the fastest on the strip, but there's something special about competing with a car that's true to its roots. It's a different kind of challenge, and it keeps me connected to the Nova's history."

The world of Nova racing is as diverse as it is exciting. From all-out drag strip monsters to lovingly preserved stock racers, these cars continue to prove their worth on tracks across the nation. The stories of triumph, the constant pursuit of faster times, and the camaraderie among Nova racers all contribute to the rich tapestry of the model's racing heritage.

As Tom Rodriguez puts it, "Racing a Nova isn't just about winning. It's about being part of a legacy, pushing the limits of what these amazing cars can do, and sharing that passion with a community of like-minded enthusiasts. Every time I fire up that engine at the starting line, I'm not just racing – I'm carrying on a tradition that's been alive for generations."

Section 8.5: Daily Drivers and Weekend Warriors

The Chevy II Nova has always been more than just a showpiece; for many enthusiasts, it's a faithful companion on the road, serving as both a daily driver and a weekend cruiser. This section examines the experiences of individuals who have chosen to integrate their classic Novas into their daily lives, striking a balance between preservation and practicality.

Chevy II Nova: Power, Passion, and Performance

Using a Nova as a daily driver in modern times presents unique challenges and rewards. Many owners speak of the satisfaction they feel piloting their vintage vehicles through contemporary traffic, standing out amidst a sea of modern cars. John Anderson, a Nova owner from Ohio, shares, "There's something special about starting my day behind the wheel of my '66 Nova. It turns heads and starts conversations wherever I go. Sure, it doesn't have all the modern amenities, but that's part of its charm."

Adapting a classic Nova for today's driving conditions often requires careful consideration and some strategic upgrades. Owners frequently mention improvements in braking systems, enhanced cooling for stop-and-go traffic, and upgraded electrical systems to accommodate modern accessories such as phone chargers and improved lighting. Sarah Martinez, who daily drives her '72 Nova in Los Angeles, explains, "I've added disc brakes and a more efficient radiator to handle the city's traffic. It's a balance between keeping the car's integrity and making it safe and reliable for everyday use."

Weekend cruises and road trips in a classic Nova offer a unique experience altogether. The open road becomes an invitation to step back in time, with the Nova's vintage feel enhanced by scenic routes and nostalgic destinations. Mark Thompson, who regularly takes his '68 Nova on weekend trips, describes the experience: "There's nothing like hitting the back roads on a Saturday morning, the rumble of the engine, and the feel of the wheel in your hands. It's not just transportation; it's time travel."

The public's reaction to seeing a Nova on the road is overwhelmingly positive. Owners report frequent thumbs-up, waves, and even occasional applause from pedestrians and fellow drivers. Gas stations become impromptu car shows, with curious onlookers asking questions and sharing their own Nova memories. This public enthusiasm often reinforces owners' commitment to keeping their cars on the road.

Maintaining a balance between preservation and usability is a constant consideration for Nova owners who frequently use their cars. Many adopt a "sympathetic modernization" approach, making subtle upgrades that improve reliability and safety without compromising the car's classic appearance. Popular modifications include electronic ignition systems, upgraded suspension components, and modern tire compounds that provide better grip and longevity.

Lisa Hernandez, who has daily driven her '74 Nova for over a decade, sums up the experience: "It's not always easy or convenient, but driving my Nova every day connects me to the car's history and to a simpler time. The extra effort it sometimes requires is more than offset by the joy it brings, not just to me, but to everyone who sees it on the road."

The stories of Nova daily drivers and weekend warriors highlight the versatility and enduring appeal of these classic cars. Whether navigating rush-hour traffic or cruising down a scenic highway, these Novas continue to fulfill their original purpose as reliable and enjoyable automobiles, while simultaneously serving as rolling ambassadors of automotive history. The owners who choose to use their Novas regularly are not just preserving these cars; they're keeping the spirit of an entire era alive on today's roads.

Section 8.6: The Nova as a Business

The Chevrolet Nova's enduring popularity has given rise to a thriving ecosystem of businesses catering to enthusiasts, collectors, and restorers. This section examines how the Nova has evolved into more than just a beloved classic car; it has become a foundation for entrepreneurship and economic activity within the automotive industry.

Nova-focused restoration shops have carved out a unique niche in the classic car industry. These specialized businesses have become go-to destinations for Nova owners seeking expert care for their prized possessions. One such shop, "Nova Nation Restorations" in Michigan, has been dedicated solely to Novas for over two decades. Owner Mike Thompson shares, "When we started, people thought we were crazy to focus on just one model. But the demand has been incredible. We've restored over 500 Novas, and there's no sign of slowing down."

The world of Nova collecting has also become a lucrative business for some. Savvy investors have recognized the potential of these classic cars as appreciating assets. John Ramirez, a California-based collector, explains, "I started buying Novas in the '90s when prices were reasonable. Now, some of the rarer models have quadrupled in value. It's not just a hobby, it's a solid investment strategy." Ramirez's collection of pristine Novas has become a multi-million dollar portfolio, demonstrating the financial potential of these classic Chevrolets.

The market for Nova parts and accessories has experienced significant growth in recent years, driven by the needs of both restorers and modifiers. Companies like "Classic Nova Supply" have built successful businesses by manufacturing and distributing both reproduction and performance parts. Sarah Lee, CEO of Classic Nova Supply, notes, "We started in our garage, making a few hard-to-find trim pieces. Now we offer over 5,000 Nova-specific parts and ship worldwide. The community's passion fuels our growth."

Success stories abound in the Nova-based business world. "Nova Nutz," a YouTube channel dedicated to Nova restoration tips and tricks, has grown from a hobby into a full-time career for its creator, Tom Wilkins. "I never imagined I could make a living sharing my love for Novas," Wilkins admits. "But with over a million subscribers and sponsorships from major parts manufacturers, it's become a dream come true."

The economic impact of the Nova on the classic car industry is substantial. From specialized insurance providers to custom upholstery shops, the ripple effect of Nova enthusiasm supports a wide range of businesses. Annual Nova-specific events, such as the "Super Nova Nationals," attract thousands of attendees, boosting local economies and showcasing the model's enduring appeal.

The Nova's business potential extends beyond restoration and parts. Nova-themed merchandise, from t-shirts to home decor, has found a receptive market. "Nova Nostalgia," an online retailer, has successfully tapped into this demand. Founder Lisa Chen explains, "We sell everything from Nova-shaped bottle openers to high-end art prints. It's amazing how many people want to showcase their Nova love in every aspect of their lives."

As the Nova approaches its 60th anniversary, the business opportunities surrounding this iconic car show no signs of waning. The increasing rarity of original examples and the growing nostalgia for classic American muscle cars suggest that the Nova-based economy will continue to thrive. From small-scale parts fabricators to extensive restoration facilities, the Chevy Nova has proven to be not just a car but a catalyst for entrepreneurship and a cornerstone of the classic car industry.

Section 8.7: Nova Clubs and Communities

The Chevy II Nova has not only captured the hearts of individual enthusiasts but has also fostered a vibrant community of like-minded individuals. This section delves into the world of Nova clubs and communities, exploring how these groups have become the backbone of Nova preservation and celebration.

Nova enthusiast clubs began forming shortly after the model's introduction, with early adopters recognizing the need for a support network. As the years passed, these clubs grew in both size and number, spanning across the United States and even internationally. Today, there are dozens of Nova-specific clubs, each with its own unique flavor but all united by their passion for this iconic vehicle.

Chevy II Nova: Power, Passion, and Performance

Annual meetups and events centered around the Nova have become highlights of the automotive calendar for many enthusiasts. These gatherings range from small, local cruise-ins to large-scale national conventions. The Nova Nationals, for instance, draws hundreds of Nova owners and thousands of spectators each year. These events serve not only as showcases for pristine restorations and creative modifications but also as invaluable networking opportunities where friendships are forged and knowledge is shared.

The digital age has revolutionized the way Nova communities connect and interact with one another. Online forums, social media groups, and dedicated websites have become treasure troves of information for Nova owners. Whether someone needs help troubleshooting an engine issue, is searching for a rare part, or simply wants to share photos of their latest project, these online communities provide instant access to a global network of experts and enthusiasts. Websites like NovaResource.com and ChevyNova.com have become go-to destinations for technical information, while Facebook groups allow for real-time discussions and photo sharing.

One of the most inspiring aspects of Nova communities is their commitment to collaborative restoration projects. It's not uncommon for club members to band together to help a fellow enthusiast bring their Nova back to life. These projects often become learning experiences for all involved, with more experienced members passing down their knowledge to newer enthusiasts. Some clubs have even taken on the restoration of Novas to be raffled off for charity, combining their passion with a greater cause.

Nova clubs play a crucial role in preserving the model's history and knowledge. Many clubs maintain archives of original documentation, rare photographs, and even hard-to-find parts and artifacts. They often work closely with museums and automotive historians to ensure that the Nova's legacy is accurately recorded and shared with future generations. Through newsletters, websites, and social media, these clubs disseminate historical information, keeping the Nova's rich history alive and relevant.

The impact of these communities extends beyond just maintaining cars. They've created a support system that spans generations, with older members mentoring younger enthusiasts and passing down not just knowledge, but a passion for the Nova as well. This intergenerational connection ensures that the Nova community continues to thrive, even as the cars themselves become older.

Nova clubs and communities have also played a crucial role in advocating for the interests of classic car owners in general. They often engage with legislators on issues affecting classic car ownership, such as emissions regulations and the availability of period-correct parts.

In essence, Nova clubs and communities have transformed what could have been a solitary hobby into a rich, shared experience. They've created a space where the love for a particular car model has blossomed into lifelong friendships, learning opportunities, and a shared sense of purpose. As one Nova club president put it, "We came for the cars, but we stayed for the people."

The story of Nova clubs and communities is a testament to the enduring appeal of the Chevy II Nova. It's not just about preserving metal and rubber; it's about keeping alive a piece of automotive history and the passion it inspires. As long as Nova enthusiasts are willing to share their knowledge, experiences, and camaraderie, the spirit of this beloved car will continue to thrive for generations to come.

Chapter 9: Restoration Nation: The Art of Bringing Novas Back to Life

Section 9.1: The Rising Popularity of Nova Restoration

In recent years, the classic car restoration scene has witnessed a remarkable surge in the popularity of Chevy II Nova projects. This iconic American muscle car, once a common sight on streets across the nation, has now become a prized possession for both automotive enthusiasts and collectors.

The nostalgia factor plays a significant role in driving this restoration trend. Many Nova enthusiasts fondly recall these cars from their youth, whether it was their first car, their parents' daily driver, or the dream machine they coveted but couldn't afford at the time. Now, with the means and opportunity to fulfill those long-held desires, they're diving headfirst into restoration projects, rekindling memories, and preserving a piece of their personal history.

The increasing value of restored Novas in the classic car market has also contributed to their rising popularity. As pristine examples become rarer, well-restored Novas are commanding impressive prices at auctions and in private sales. This appreciation in value not only justifies the time and expense invested in restoration but also attracts investors looking for tangible assets with growth potential. The Nova's relatively compact size and straightforward mechanics make it an attractive option for both seasoned restorers and newcomers to the classic car scene.

Restoring a Nova presents a unique blend of challenge and reward that appeals to many automotive enthusiasts. The process of bringing a neglected or worn-out Nova back to its former glory requires dedication, skill, and patience. From sourcing rare parts to mastering period-correct restoration techniques, each step of the journey tests the restorer's abilities. However, the sense of accomplishment that comes with completing a Nova restoration project is unparalleled. The transformation from a rusted relic to a gleaming showpiece is a testament to the restorer's craftsmanship and perseverance.

As more enthusiasts embark on Nova restoration projects, a vibrant subculture has emerged within the broader classic car community. Nova-specific clubs, forums, and events have emerged across the country, offering platforms for enthusiasts to share knowledge, showcase their projects, and celebrate their shared passion. These communities foster a sense of camaraderie and support that enhances the restoration experience, turning what can often be a solitary pursuit into a collaborative effort.

The rise of social media and online forums has played a crucial role in connecting Nova restorers across geographical boundaries. Platforms like Facebook groups, Instagram, and dedicated Nova restoration forums have become invaluable resources for enthusiasts. Here, restorers can seek advice on challenging aspects of their projects, share progress updates, and even locate hard-to-find parts. The ability to instantly connect with fellow Nova enthusiasts around the world has not only accelerated the learning curve for many restorers but has also helped preserve and disseminate crucial knowledge about these classic vehicles.

As the Nova restoration movement continues to gain momentum, it's clear that this isn't just a passing trend. It represents a deep-seated appreciation for American automotive heritage and a desire to keep these rolling pieces of history alive for future generations. Whether driven by nostalgia, investment potential, or pure passion for the craft, Nova restorers are ensuring that these beloved classics will continue to turn heads and ignite imaginations for years to come.

Section 9.2: Planning Your Nova Restoration Project

Embarking on a Nova restoration project is an exciting journey, but like any significant undertaking, proper planning is crucial for success. Before you dive into the details of the restoration process, it's essential to lay a solid foundation for your project.

The first step in planning your Nova restoration is to assess the condition of your vehicle thoroughly. This evaluation will help you set realistic goals for the project. Take the time to carefully inspect every aspect of the car, from the body and frame to the engine and interior. Document your findings, noting areas that require minor repairs, major overhauls, or complete replacements. This detailed assessment will serve as a roadmap for your restoration journey, helping you prioritize tasks effectively.

Once you have a clear understanding of your Nova's condition, it's time to dive into research. Familiarize yourself with period-correct details and specifications for your specific model year. This knowledge is crucial for maintaining authenticity and historical accuracy in your restoration. Consult factory manuals, period literature, and online resources dedicated to Chevy II Novas. Pay close attention to details such as paint codes, upholstery patterns, and factory-installed options. This research will not only guide your restoration decisions but also deepen your appreciation for the Nova's rich history.

With a clear vision of your project's scope, it's time to create a budget and timeline. Restoration costs can quickly escalate, so it's essential to be realistic and include a buffer for unexpected expenses. Break down your budget into categories such as body work, mechanical restoration, interior refurbishment, and parts acquisition. As for the timeline, be generous with your estimates. Restoration projects often take longer than anticipated due to unforeseen challenges or delays in sourcing parts. Setting a realistic timeline will help manage your expectations and reduce stress throughout the process.

One of the most significant decisions you'll face is choosing between a complete restoration and a resto-mod approach. A full restoration aims to return the Nova to its original factory specifications, preserving its historical authenticity. This approach is ideal for purists and collectors who value originality above all else. On the other hand, a resto-mod combines classic aesthetics with modern technology and performance upgrades. This approach allows for improved drivability, safety, and comfort while maintaining the Nova's iconic appearance. Consider your goals, budget, and intended use for the car when making this decision.

Finally, consider building a team or network of experts to assist with your project. While many enthusiasts tackle restorations as solo projects, having access to specialized knowledge and skills can be invaluable. Connect with local Nova clubs, attend classic car events, and participate in online forums to build relationships with fellow restorers. These connections can provide advice, troubleshooting help, and even leads on hard-to-find parts. Don't hesitate to seek out professionals for complex tasks that are beyond your expertise, such as engine rebuilding or custom upholstery work.

Remember, planning your Nova restoration project is not just about logistics; it's about setting the stage for a rewarding journey. By thoroughly assessing your car, researching specifications, setting a realistic budget and timeline, deciding on your restoration approach, and building a support network, you'll be well-prepared to bring your Nova back to its former glory. With careful planning, your restoration project will not only result in a beautifully restored classic but also provide a deeply satisfying experience that connects you to the rich heritage of the Chevy II Nova.

Section 9.3: Sourcing Parts and Materials

One of the most challenging aspects of restoring a Chevy II Nova is finding the right parts and materials to bring your classic back to life. As these vehicles age, original components become increasingly scarce, making the hunt for authentic pieces a crucial part of the restoration process.

The challenge of finding original Nova parts cannot be overstated. Many components specific to these vehicles have been out of production for a long time, and those that remain are often in high demand among restorers. This scarcity has led to a thriving market for reproduction parts, but navigating this landscape requires careful consideration of quality and authenticity.

When it comes to reproduction parts, not all are created equal. Some manufacturers prioritize authenticity, meticulously recreating components to match original specifications. Others may focus on improved durability or performance, sacrificing some period-correct details in the process. As a restorer, it's essential to research and select parts that align with your restoration goals, whether you're aiming for a concours-quality showpiece or a reliable daily driver with modern upgrades.

Salvage yards and classic car swap meets remain invaluable resources for Nova enthusiasts. These venues offer the opportunity to unearth genuine parts that may be impossible to find elsewhere. The thrill of discovering a rare component in a sea of automotive history is unmatched, and many restorers consider these hunts an integral part of the restoration experience. However, patience and persistence are key, as the perfect part may not reveal itself on the first, or even the tenth, visit.

In the digital age, online resources have become indispensable for sourcing Nova-specific parts and materials. Dedicated forums, social media groups, and e-commerce platforms specializing in classic car parts have made it easier than ever to connect with fellow enthusiasts and suppliers of classic car parts worldwide. These online communities not only provide access to a vast marketplace of components but also serve as valuable sources of knowledge and advice from experienced restorers.

Throughout the sourcing process, the importance of documenting part numbers and specifications cannot be overstated. Keeping meticulous records of the components you need, those you've acquired, and their correct applications will save countless hours of frustration down the line. This documentation also proves invaluable when verifying the authenticity of your restoration, potentially increasing the value of your Nova in the classic car market.

As you embark on your parts-sourcing journey, remember that creativity and adaptability are often as important as persistence. Sometimes, the exact part you need may no longer be available, requiring you to explore alternatives or consider having a component custom-fabricated. This problem-solving aspect of restoration can be both challenging and rewarding, often leading to innovative solutions that contribute to the unique story of your Nova's rebirth.

Ultimately, sourcing parts and materials for your Nova restoration is a test of patience, resourcefulness, and dedication. It's a process that connects you not just to the physical components of your vehicle, but to the rich history and community surrounding these beloved classics. Each part you track down brings you one step closer to realizing your vision and preserving a piece of automotive heritage for future generations to appreciate.

Section 9.4: Body Work and Paint

Restoring the body and paint of a classic Chevy II Nova is often the most visually rewarding aspect of the restoration process. It's where the true transformation becomes apparent, bringing the car's original beauty back to life. This process begins with a thorough assessment of the vehicle's body condition, identifying areas of rust, dents, and other damage that need attention.

Rust is the nemesis of any classic car restorer, and Novas are no exception. Common rust-prone areas include the floor pans, trunk, and lower quarter panels. Addressing rust requires careful cutting out of the affected areas and welding in new, properly shaped metal patches. For more extensive damage, entire panels may need to be replaced. This is where the skill of an experienced body technician becomes invaluable, ensuring seamless integration of new parts with the original body.

Panel replacement and fabrication is an art form in itself. While reproduction panels are available for many parts of the Nova, some areas may require custom fabrication. This involves shaping metal to match the original contours of the car, a process that demands both skill and patience. The goal is to recreate the Nova's iconic lines while ensuring structural integrity.

Once the bodywork is complete, attention turns to the paint. Selecting the right color is crucial, especially for enthusiasts aiming for a period-correct restoration. Nova color codes from the 1960s and early 1970s can be researched to ensure authenticity. However, some restorers opt for custom colors that complement the car's lines, adding a unique flair.

The debate between modern paint technologies and period-correct finishes is ongoing in the restoration community. Modern paints offer superior durability and a wider range of color options, while period-correct finishes provide unmatched authenticity. Many restorers strike a balance by using modern base coats for durability, topped with period-correct color and clear coats for authenticity.

The painting process itself is meticulous, involving multiple stages of priming, painting, and clear coating. Each layer must be carefully applied and allowed to cure before the next is added. The result, when done correctly, is a deep, lustrous finish that looks as good as, or better than, the day the Nova rolled off the assembly line.

The final touches in body restoration involve the chrome, trim, and emblems. These elements are what truly make a Nova stand out. Original pieces can often be rechromed or polished to restore their shine. When originals are beyond repair, reproduction parts can be sourced. Attention to detail is crucial here, as the correct placement of each emblem and trim piece contributes to the overall authenticity of the restoration.

Throughout the body and paint restoration process, patience is key. Rushing can lead to subpar results that detract from the overall quality of the restoration. It's not uncommon for this phase of the project to take several months, but the result, a gleaming, perfectly finished Nova, is well worth the time and effort invested.

Section 9.5: Mechanical Restoration

The heart of any classic car restoration lies in its mechanical components, and the Chevy II Nova is no exception. Bringing these iconic machines back to life requires a delicate balance between preserving their originality and incorporating modern improvements for enhanced safety and reliability.

Engine rebuilding is often the centerpiece of mechanical restoration. For Nova enthusiasts, this process involves carefully disassembling the original powerplant, inspecting each component, and deciding what can be restored and what needs replacement. Whether you're working with the base inline-six or one of the legendary V8 options, attention to detail is crucial. Many restorers face the dilemma of maintaining stock specifications or opting for performance upgrades. The key is to strike a balance that respects the Nova's heritage while potentially enhancing its drivability.

Transmission and drivetrain overhaul is another critical aspect of mechanical restoration. Whether your Nova came equipped with a manual or automatic transmission, these components often require significant attention after decades of use. Rebuilding the transmission ensures smooth gear changes and proper power delivery. Don't forget the driveshaft, rear axle, and differential; these components are essential for transferring power to the wheels and maintaining the Nova's legendary straight-line performance.

Suspension and steering restoration is crucial for improving handling and providing a comfortable driving experience. Many Nova restorers opt to rebuild the front suspension with new bushings, ball joints, and tie rod ends. Replacing worn shocks or upgrading to modern coil-over setups can dramatically improve ride quality. Power steering, while not original to all Novas, is a popular upgrade that enhances drivability without significantly altering the car's character.

Brake system upgrades are an ordinary and often necessary modification in Nova restorations. While purists may opt to rebuild the original drum brake system, many restorers choose to upgrade to disc brakes, at the very least, on the front axle. This modification significantly improves stopping power and safety, making the Nova more suitable for modern driving conditions. When making such upgrades, it's essential to ensure that all components are correctly sized and compatible with the rest of the vehicle's systems.

Electrical system restoration is often one of the most challenging aspects of reviving a Nova. Decades-old wiring can pose a fire hazard and usually causes frustrating, intermittent issues. Many restorers opt for a complete rewiring of the vehicle, using modern materials that maintain a period-correct appearance. This is also an opportunity to upgrade the charging system, incorporating an alternator if the car originally came with a generator. Modernizing the electrical system can enhance reliability and enable the integration of modern conveniences, such as upgraded lighting or audio systems.

Throughout the mechanical restoration process, it's crucial to document every step, keeping track of part numbers, specifications, and any modifications made. This documentation not only aids in future maintenance but also adds value to the restored Nova, providing a detailed history of the work performed.

The mechanical restoration of a Chevy II Nova is a labor of love that requires patience, skill, and a deep appreciation for automotive engineering. By carefully rebuilding and upgrading these core systems, restorers can create a classic car that not only looks the part but drives like a dream, bridging the gap between vintage appeal and modern performance.

Section 9.6: Interior Restoration

The interior of a classic Chevy II Nova is where drivers and passengers alike experience the true essence of the vehicle. Restoring this space to its former glory requires a delicate balance of authenticity and functionality. Let's delve into the intricacies of interior restoration, exploring the challenges and rewards of bringing the Nova's cabin back to life.

Sourcing and restoring original upholstery is often one of the most challenging aspects of interior restoration. The materials used in vintage Novas may no longer be in production, requiring restorers to hunt for new old stock (NOS) or high-quality reproductions. For those lucky enough to find original seat covers and door panels, careful cleaning and repair can breathe new life into these pieces.

However, many restorers opt for custom-made upholstery that mimics the original patterns and materials. This approach enables improved durability while preserving the classic look.

The dashboard and instrument cluster are focal points of the Nova's interior and deserve special attention. Often, these components suffer from years of sun damage and wear and tear. Restoring the dashboard may involve repairing cracks, refinishing surfaces, and replacing worn-out gauges. Some restorers choose to have their instrument clusters professionally refurbished, ensuring that all gauges function correctly and maintain their vintage appearance. The attention to detail in this area can make or break the overall authenticity of the restoration.

Restoring or replacing interior trim and detailing is a meticulous process that can truly elevate the final result. This includes items such as the steering wheel, shifter knob, pedal covers, and various plastic or metal trim pieces. Many of these items can be refurbished through careful cleaning and polishing, while others may require replacement with reproduction parts. The key is to maintain consistency in finish and color across all components, creating a cohesive and period-correct look.

While staying true to the original design is essential, many Nova enthusiasts opt for modern comfort upgrades while maintaining a vintage look. This might include subtle additions such as improved sound insulation, more comfortable seat padding, or even discreetly installed air conditioning. The challenge lies in integrating these modern comforts without compromising the classic aesthetic. Skilled restorers can often find creative ways to hide modern conveniences, ensuring that the Nova's interior remains true to its era at first glance.

Audio system options present another opportunity to strike a balance between historical accuracy and modern technology. For purists, restoring the original AM radio to working condition might be the goal. However, many restorers opt for modern sound systems that offer improved quality and features. The key is to choose components that can be hidden or designed to look period-correct. Some companies even provide classic-looking radio faces that house modern internals, allowing for features like Bluetooth connectivity without disrupting the vintage dashboard appearance.

Throughout the interior restoration process, attention to detail is paramount. Every knob, switch, and lever should be carefully considered and restored or replaced as needed. The headliner, sun visors, and even the dome light all play a role in creating an authentic and immersive classic car experience.

It's worth noting that interior restoration also presents an opportunity for personalization. While some restorers aim for factory-original interiors, others use this as a chance to create a unique space that reflects their personal style while still honoring the Nova's heritage. This might involve custom color schemes, bespoke upholstery patterns, or even the integration of modern gauges designed to look period-correct.

Ultimately, a well-restored Nova interior should transport occupants back in time, offering a tactile connection to the car's history. It should feel authentic, comfortable, and cohesive, with every element working together to create an immersive classic car experience. The process of interior restoration, while challenging, offers an enriching opportunity to preserve and enhance the character of these beloved classics, ensuring that future generations can experience the Chevy II Nova just as it was in its heyday.

Section 9.7: The Final Touches and Debut

As your Nova restoration project nears completion, the excitement builds for the final touches and the much-anticipated debut. This stage is where your hard work, dedication, and attention to detail truly shine.

The process begins with final detailing and polishing. Every surface of your restored Nova receives meticulous attention. The paint is carefully buffed to a mirror-like finish, bringing out the depth and luster of the color. Chrome trim is polished to a brilliant shine, and every nook and cranny is cleaned to perfection. This is the time to address those slight imperfections that may have been overlooked earlier, ensuring that your Nova looks its absolute best.

With the aesthetics perfected, it's time for road testing and fine-tuning. This crucial step allows you to identify and address any mechanical issues that may have arisen during the restoration process. It's not uncommon to discover minor adjustments that need to be made, whether it's tweaking the carburetor for optimal performance or adjusting the suspension for the perfect ride. These test drives also serve as a thrilling preview of what's to come, as you experience the fruits of your labor firsthand.

Documentation and certification of the restoration are often-overlooked but necessary steps. Keeping detailed records of the restoration process, including before-and-after photos, parts receipts, and notes on modifications or repairs, adds value to your Nova and provides a comprehensive history for future owners. For particularly high-end restorations, consider having your Nova certified by a recognized classic car authority, which can significantly increase its value and appeal to collectors.

The moment you've been waiting for finally arrives: unveiling your restored Nova at car shows and events. This is your opportunity to showcase your hard work and craftsmanship to fellow enthusiasts and the public. The pride you'll feel as onlookers admire your Nova is indescribable. Be prepared to answer questions about your restoration process and to share stories about the challenges you overcame. These events are not just about displaying your car; they're about connecting with a community that shares your passion for classic Novas.

The most rewarding aspect of completing a Nova restoration project is the emotional satisfaction it brings. There's an unparalleled sense of accomplishment in getting a piece of automotive history back to life. Every time you slide behind the wheel or simply gaze at your restored Nova in the garage, you'll be reminded of the journey you've undertaken. The countless hours of work, problem-solving, moments of frustration, and breakthroughs all culminate in this beautiful machine before you.

Your restored Nova is more than just a car; it's a testament to your dedication, skill, and love for automotive history. It represents a connection to the past and a preservation of America's rich car culture. As you drive your Nova down the street, turning heads and evoking smiles from passersby, you'll know that you've done more than just restore a car; you've kept a piece of history alive for future generations to appreciate and enjoy.

Chapter 10: Nova vs. The World: Comparing the Chevy II to Its Rivals

Section 10.1: The Muscle Car Arena

The 1960s and early 1970s marked the golden age of American muscle cars, a period characterized by high-performance vehicles that captivated the imagination of both car enthusiasts and casual drivers. This era was defined by a potent mix of powerful engines, aggressive styling, and an undeniable aura of coolness that permeated popular culture.

At the heart of the muscle car phenomenon were several key players, each vying for supremacy on the streets and in the showrooms. Giants like Ford, Chevrolet, Pontiac, and Dodge led the charge, producing iconic models that would become legends in their own right. The Mustang, Camaro, GTO, and Charger were just a few of the names that became synonymous with American automotive prowess.

A unique set of factors drove the market dynamics of this period. Post-war prosperity had created a generation of young buyers with disposable income and a thirst for excitement. These consumers weren't just looking for transportation; they wanted vehicles that made a statement. Performance was paramount, with quarter-mile times and horsepower figures becoming the currency of choice among enthusiasts.

But it wasn't just about raw power. Style played an equally crucial role in the muscle car equation. Aggressive lines, bold colors, and eye-catching details were essential in catching the attention of potential buyers. The aesthetics of these vehicles reflected the times, bold, optimistic, and unapologetically American.

Affordability was another key factor in the muscle car wars. Manufacturers worked tirelessly to strike the perfect balance between performance and price, aiming to deliver maximum thrills without breaking the bank. This focus on value led to innovations in engineering and manufacturing, as companies sought ways to extract ever more power from increasingly efficient and cost-effective designs.

Brand loyalty played a significant role in the muscle car market. Many buyers had strong allegiances to particular manufacturers, often influenced by family traditions or regional preferences. The fierce competition between brands only served to strengthen these loyalties, with fans of Ford, Chevy, and Mopar engaging in heated debates about the merits of their preferred marques.

Perhaps the most defining characteristic of the muscle car era was the concept of "bang for your buck." This idea perfectly encapsulated the American spirit of the time, the belief that performance and excitement should be accessible to the masses, not just the wealthy elite. Muscle cars offered ordinary people the chance to own a piece of the American dream, a vehicle that could hold its own against much more expensive sports cars while still being practical enough for daily use.

It was into this arena that the Chevy II Nova stepped, ready to make its mark. As we'll see in the following sections, the Nova would prove to be a formidable contender, combining performance, style, and value in a package that would challenge its rivals and win the hearts of many American drivers. The stage was set for a showdown that would help define an era and leave an indelible mark on automotive history.

Section 10.2: Nova vs. Ford Falcon

The Chevrolet Nova and the Ford Falcon were two of the most prominent compact cars that evolved into muscle car contenders during the 1960s and early 1970s. Both had humble beginnings as economy-minded family cars before embracing the performance ethos of the era.

The Nova, initially badged as the Chevy II, and the Falcon were introduced in the early 1960s as responses to the growing demand for smaller, more efficient vehicles. The Falcon hit the market first in 1960, followed by the Chevy II in 1962. Initially, both cars were positioned as practical and affordable alternatives to full-sized sedans, targeting budget-conscious consumers and growing families.

As the muscle car craze took hold, both Ford and Chevrolet recognized the potential to transform these compact platforms into high-performance machines. The Nova, particularly in its Super Sport (SS) guise, offered a range of potent V8 engines, including the legendary 350- and 396-cubic-inch powerplants. The Falcon, while never receiving a dedicated performance badge like the SS, could be optioned with Ford's robust 289 and later 302 V8 engines.

In terms of performance, the Nova generally had the edge. The Nova SS, especially when equipped with the 396 big-block V8, was a formidable straight-line performer, capable of quarter-mile times that rivaled many of its larger muscle car brethren. The Falcon, while quick in its own right, typically couldn't match the Nova's top-end performance options.

Styling-wise, the two cars took different approaches. The Nova, particularly in its second generation, embraced a more muscular, aggressive look with a long hood and short deck proportions that screamed "performance." The Falcon, on the other hand, maintained a somewhat more conservative appearance throughout its lifespan, even as it adopted more performance-oriented features.

Sales figures and market reception for both models were strong, but the Nova ultimately proved to have more staying power. While the Falcon name was discontinued in the U.S. market after 1970 (surviving in the form of the Ford Maverick), the Nova remained a strong seller for Chevrolet well into the 1970s. This longevity allowed the Nova to become more deeply ingrained in muscle car culture.

The long-term legacy of both models is significant, albeit in different ways. The Falcon's importance lies primarily in its role as the foundation for the Ford Mustang, one of the most iconic muscle cars of all time. The Nova, however, became a legend in its own right, particularly in its SS form. It remains a highly sought-after collector car and a popular choice for restoration and modification projects.

In the annals of muscle car history, both the Nova and the Falcon played crucial roles. They demonstrated that high performance wasn't limited to full-sized cars and helped democratize the muscle car experience. However, the Nova's more extensive performance options, longer production run, and stronger association with the muscle car ethos have cemented its place as the more iconic muscle machine of the two.

Section 10.3: Nova vs. Plymouth Valiant

The Chevrolet Nova and Plymouth Valiant shared humble beginnings as compact cars before evolving into formidable muscle machines. Both models emerged in the early 1960s as automakers sought to capture the growing market for smaller, more economical vehicles. The Valiant, introduced in 1960, predated the Nova (initially branded as the Chevy II) by two years, giving Plymouth a slight head start in establishing its compact car credentials.

As the decade progressed, both cars underwent a remarkable transformation, mirroring the shifting preferences of American consumers towards more powerful and sporty vehicles. The Nova, particularly in its Super Sport (SS) guise, and the Valiant, especially when equipped with high-performance options, began to shed their image as economy cars and embrace the muscle car ethos.

Performance capabilities became a key battleground between these two rivals. Chevrolet offered the Nova with a range of potent engines, including the legendary 350 cubic inch V8, which could propel the car from 0 to 60 mph in under 7 seconds. Plymouth countered with its own array of powerplants, most notably the 273 cubic-inch LA V8 and later, the more robust 340 cubic-inch V8. These engines gave the Valiant, particularly in its sportier Duster variant, the muscle to go toe-to-toe with the Nova on the street and the strip.

While both cars could be outfitted with serious horsepower, they approached the market with slightly different value propositions. The Nova, benefiting from Chevrolet's extensive dealer network and brand recognition, often commanded a slight premium over its competitors. However, it also offered a wider range of options and trim levels, allowing buyers to tailor their purchase more precisely to their needs and budget. The Valiant, on the other hand, often undercut the Nova in base price, positioning itself as a more affordable entry point into the world of compact muscle cars.

Brand perception and marketing strategies played a crucial role in the rivalry between these two models. Chevrolet leveraged its strong performance heritage, tying the Nova to its broader muscle car lineup that included icons like the Camaro and Chevelle. This association lent the Nova an air of performance credibility that resonated with enthusiasts. Plymouth, part of the Chrysler Corporation, took a different tack. They often marketed the Valiant (and its performance variants) as clever alternatives to the mainstream choices, appealing to buyers who wanted to stand out from the crowd.

The Nova and Valiant's competition extended beyond the showroom floor and onto the streets and drag strips of America. Both cars developed strong followings among performance enthusiasts, who appreciated their combination of compact size, relatively light weight, and potent engines. This grassroots support helped cement the reputations of both models as legitimate muscle cars, despite their more modest origins.

As the muscle car era progressed, both the Nova and Valiant demonstrated remarkable adaptability. They managed to maintain their appeal even as changing regulations and shifting consumer preferences began to impact the broader muscle car market. This flexibility would prove crucial in extending their production runs and ensuring their places in automotive history.

Ultimately, the rivalry between the Chevrolet Nova and the Plymouth Valiant epitomized the spirit of the muscle car era. Both cars proved that high performance wasn't limited to full-size models or premium brands. They brought the thrill of powerful V8 engines and spirited driving to a broader audience, all while maintaining a degree of practicality that made them usable as daily drivers. This blend of performance and pragmatism ensured that both the Nova and Valiant would be remembered not just as participants in the muscle car phenomenon but as significant contributors to its enduring legacy.

Section 10.4: Nova vs. Pontiac GTO

When discussing the muscle car era, it's impossible to ignore the impact of the Pontiac GTO. Often considered the quintessential muscle car, the GTO set a high bar for performance and style. The

Chevy II Nova: Power, Passion, and Performance

Chevy II Nova, particularly in its SS guise, found itself in direct competition with this automotive legend.

The Pontiac GTO, introduced in 1964, was a game-changer in the automotive world. It combined a powerful V8 engine with a mid-size body, creating a formula that would define the muscle car category. The Nova SS, while slightly smaller, aimed to capture the same spirit of accessible performance.

In terms of raw power, the GTO initially had the upper hand. Its standard 389 cubic inch V8 engine produced an impressive 325 horsepower, with options pushing that figure even higher. The Nova SS, starting with a 283 cubic inch V8 making 195 horsepower, was clearly outgunned at first. However, Chevrolet quickly responded to market demands, offering larger engines in subsequent years, including the formidable 396 cubic-inch big-block V8, which could produce up to 375 horsepower. This engine option allowed the Nova SS to close the performance gap significantly.

Despite the Nova's impressive power upgrades, the GTO maintained an edge in straight-line acceleration due to its weight distribution and purpose-built performance design. However, the Nova SS often proved more nimble in handling, thanks to its lighter weight and shorter wheelbase. This made the Nova a favorite among drivers who appreciated a balance of straight-line speed and cornering ability.

When it came to price points, the Nova SS held a clear advantage. As a smaller car with more modest base trim levels, it offered an accessible entry point into the world of high performance. The GTO, positioned as a premium muscle car, commanded a higher price tag. This pricing strategy enabled the Nova SS to appeal to a broader demographic, including younger buyers and those seeking a practical car with a performance edge.

Chevy II Nova: Power, Passion, and Performance

The target demographics for these two cars often overlapped but had distinct differences. The GTO typically attracted buyers seeking a pure muscle car experience, usually those willing to sacrifice some practicality for style and performance. The Nova SS, on the other hand, appealed to buyers who wanted the thrills of a muscle car without completely sacrificing the practicality of a smaller, more efficient vehicle.

In popular culture, both cars left their mark, but in different ways. The GTO became an icon of the muscle car era, frequently featured in movies, TV shows, and music of the time. It was the car that epitomized American performance and excess. The Nova, while also making numerous pop culture appearances, often played a different role. It was frequently portrayed as the underdog, the sleeper that could surprise flashier cars at the stoplight. This image resonated with many enthusiasts who appreciated the Nova's blend of unassuming looks and potent performance.

The impact on their respective brands was significant. For Pontiac, the GTO solidified the division's performance image, paving the way for a series of legendary muscle cars. It transformed Pontiac's brand identity, pushing it towards a more youthful, performance-oriented image. The Nova, while not as transformative for Chevrolet's overall brand, played a crucial role in broadening the appeal of performance cars within the Chevrolet lineup. It showed that Chevrolet could offer exciting performance options across various vehicle sizes and price points, from the compact Nova to the mid-size Chevelle and full-size Impala.

In conclusion, while the Pontiac GTO may have defined the muscle car era, the Chevy II Nova SS proved to be a worthy competitor. It offered a unique blend of performance, practicality, and affordability, allowing it to carve out its own niche in the highly competitive muscle car market. The Nova SS demonstrated that high performance wasn't just for premium brands or larger cars, helping to democratize the muscle car experience for a broader range of enthusiasts.

Section 10.5: Nova vs. Dodge Dart

The Chevrolet Nova and the Dodge Dart shared a similar trajectory in the automotive world, both evolving from modest compact cars into formidable muscle machines. This transformation reflected the changing tastes of American consumers and the escalating horsepower wars of the 1960s and early 1970s.

Initially introduced as economy-minded compact cars, both the Nova and the Dart underwent significant transformations to appeal to performance enthusiasts. The Nova's journey from the practical Chevy II to the muscular Nova SS mirrored the Dart's evolution from a sensible family car to the performance-oriented Dart GTS and Swinger models. This parallel development showcased the adaptability of both Chevrolet and Dodge in responding to market demands.

When it came to engine options and performance capabilities, both cars offered a range of choices to suit various drivers. The Nova SS could be equipped with engines ranging from the robust 327 cubic inch V8 to the tire-shredding 396 big block. Similarly, the Dart GTS offered Chrysler's renowned 383- and 440-cubic-inch engines. The ultimate expression of Dart performance was the limited-production 426 Hemi option, which gave the Dart a slight edge in raw power. However, the Nova's broader range of engine choices provided buyers with more flexibility to balance performance and practicality.

In terms of styling and design elements, the Nova and Dart took different approaches. The Nova embraced a cleaner, more understated design that aged gracefully over time. Its simple lines and uncluttered appearance gave it a timeless quality that many enthusiasts appreciate to this day. The Dart, particularly in its performance trims, adopted a more aggressive stance with bold styling cues like hood scoops and prominent striping. This more extroverted appearance appealed to buyers looking to make a strong visual statement.

Marketing approaches and brand positioning also differed between the two models. Chevrolet positioned the Nova as a versatile vehicle that could be anything from an economical daily driver to a weekend warrior at the drag strip. This broad appeal allowed the Nova to capture a wide segment of the market. Dodge, on the other hand, more explicitly targeted performance enthusiasts with the Dart GTS and Swinger models, emphasizing their racing pedigree and connection to Dodge's larger muscle cars, such as the Charger.

Both the Nova and the Dart demonstrated remarkable adaptability to changing market conditions. As emissions regulations tightened and fuel prices rose in the early 1970s, both models were able to pivot back towards their economical roots while still maintaining a performance edge. The Nova's diverse platform allowed it to weather these changes particularly well, offering fuel-efficient six-cylinder options alongside its V8 powerplants. The Dart, while also adaptable, began to focus more on its compact car identity as the muscle car era waned.

In the end, the competition between the Nova and the Dart exemplified the intense rivalry between American automakers during this golden age of performance. While the Dart may have had a slight edge in ultimate performance with its Hemi option, the Nova's broader appeal and adaptability helped cement its place in automotive history. Both cars left an indelible mark on the muscle car era, showcasing the ingenuity and competitive spirit of their respective manufacturers.

Section 10.6: The Nova's Unique Selling Points

While the Chevy II Nova faced stiff competition in the muscle car era, it possessed several unique selling points that set it apart from its rivals. One of the Nova's greatest strengths was its ability to strike a perfect balance between performance and practicality. Unlike some of its more extreme muscle car counterparts, the Nova offered impressive power without sacrificing everyday usability. This made it an attractive option for buyers who wanted the thrill of a high-performance vehicle but also needed a car that could serve as reliable daily transportation.

Chevrolet's extensive dealer network played a crucial role in the success of the Nova. With dealerships spread across the country, potential buyers had easy access to sales, service, and parts. This widespread availability not only made the Nova more accessible to a broader range of customers but also provided peace of mind regarding long-term maintenance and support.

The Nova's broad appeal across different buyer segments was another key advantage. Its versatile platform allowed it to cater to a wide range of tastes and needs. From budget-conscious buyers looking for a stylish compact to performance enthusiasts seeking a potent muscle car, the Nova had something to offer. This adaptability allowed Chevrolet to cast a wide net in the market, attracting a diverse customer base that contributed to the model's enduring popularity.

Reliability was another feather in the Nova's cap. While some muscle cars gained reputations for being temperamental or high-maintenance, the Nova stood out for its dependability. Built on a proven platform and utilizing well-established Chevrolet mechanicals, the Nova offered a level of reliability that many buyers found reassuring. This reputation for durability not only attracted initial buyers but also contributed to the Nova's substantial resale value and long-term desirability.

One of the Nova's most significant unique selling points was its adaptability to aftermarket modifications. The car's simple, robust design and readily available Chevrolet small-block V8 engines made it a favorite among hot rodders and performance enthusiasts. Owners could easily upgrade their Novas with a wide range of performance parts, allowing for customization and increased power output. This modifiability extended the Nova's appeal beyond its stock configurations, creating a thriving aftermarket industry and cementing its status as a performance icon.

The combination of these unique selling points, performance balanced with practicality, widespread availability, broad market appeal, reputation for reliability, and ease of modification, created a compelling package that set the Nova apart in a crowded field. These factors not only contributed to its success during its production run but also helped explain its enduring popularity among classic car enthusiasts today. The Nova wasn't just another muscle car; it was a versatile, accessible, and reliable performance machine that captured the essence of the era while offering something for nearly everyone.

Section 10.7: Legacy and Collector's Perspective

The Chevy II Nova's impact extends far beyond its production years, leaving an indelible mark on the collector car market and American automotive culture. Today, the Nova stands as a testament to the golden age of muscle cars, with its value and desirability among enthusiasts continuing to grow.

In the current collector market, the Nova holds its own against its period rivals. While it may not command the astronomical prices of some rarer muscle cars, well-preserved or restored Novas, particularly SS models, fetch impressive sums at auctions. The Nova's value proposition remains strong, often offering more bang for the buck compared to some of its contemporaries. This accessibility has made it a popular choice for collectors looking to enter the classic muscle car market without breaking the bank.

One of the Nova's greatest strengths in the collector world is the availability of parts and the relative ease of restoration. Thanks to its popularity and Chevrolet's extensive production, a vast aftermarket has developed to support Nova enthusiasts. From body panels to engine components, restorers can find virtually every part needed to bring a Nova back to its former glory. This abundance of parts not only makes restoration projects more feasible but also helps keep maintenance costs manageable for collectors.

The Nova's enduring popularity is evident at car shows and enthusiast events nationwide. Its compact size, powerful engine options, and classic styling make it a crowd-pleaser at gatherings of all sizes. Nova owners' clubs and model-specific events have sprung up nationwide, fostering a vibrant community of enthusiasts who share knowledge, parts, and a passion for these iconic cars.

Several unique features make the Nova stand out to collectors. Its "sleeper" status, the ability to pack serious performance into an unassuming package, continues to captivate enthusiasts. The variety of engine options and trim levels means there's a Nova to suit almost every collector's taste, from mild to wild. Additionally, the Nova's rich racing heritage, particularly in drag racing, adds to its allure for performance-minded collectors.

The long-term impact of the Nova on American car culture cannot be overstated. It represents a pivotal moment in automotive history when performance became accessible to the masses. The Nova's influence is evident in the design and marketing of subsequent generations of compact performance cars. Its legacy lives on not just in pristine examples in climate-controlled garages, but in the countless Nova-inspired hot rods and customs that grace streets and drag strips across America.

As time passes, the Nova's place in the pantheon of great American muscle cars becomes ever more secure. It serves as a rolling history lesson, a reminder of an era when Detroit iron ruled the roads and performance was king. For collectors and enthusiasts, the Chevy II Nova is more than just a car; it's a piece of automotive Americana, a tangible link to a bygone era that continues to captivate and inspire new generations of car enthusiasts.

Chevy II Nova: Power, Passion, and Performance

Chapter 11: Collecting Nostalgia: The Nova in Today's Classic Car Market

Section 11.1: The Nova's Rise in the Collector Car Market

The Chevy II Nova's journey from an everyday vehicle to a coveted collector's item is a testament to its enduring appeal and cultural significance. Over the past few decades, this unassuming compact car has experienced a remarkable ascent in the classic car market, captivating enthusiasts and investors alike.

Tracing the Nova's market trajectory reveals a fascinating story of appreciation. In the 1980s, these cars were often overlooked, with even well-maintained examples changing hands for just a few thousand dollars. Fast forward to today, and the landscape has undergone a dramatic shift. Pristine Novas, particularly those from sought-after model years or with desirable options, can now command six-figure sums at auction. This meteoric rise in value reflects not just inflation, but a growing recognition of the Nova's place in automotive history.

Chevy II Nova: Power, Passion, and Performance

Several factors have contributed to the Nova's increasing collectibility. First and foremost is rarity, especially for specific models and configurations. The 1966-67 Chevy II Nova SS, for instance, has become particularly coveted due to its limited production numbers and powerful engine options. These cars represent the peak of Nova performance during the muscle car era, making them highly desirable to collectors who prize both style and substance.

Historical significance also plays a crucial role in the Nova's collector appeal. As a key player in the compact car revolution of the 1960s and a participant in the muscle car wars that followed, the Nova holds an essential place in automotive lore. Its evolution from an economical family car to a street performance machine mirrors the changing automotive landscape of mid-century America, giving it a broader cultural resonance.

When compared to other muscle cars in the classic car market, the Nova occupies a unique position. While it may not command the same astronomical prices as some of its more famous contemporaries, such as the Mustang or Camaro, the Nova offers collectors a compelling blend of performance, style, and relative affordability. This accessibility has actually worked in its favor, attracting a diverse range of enthusiasts and maintaining high interest across various market segments.

Generational nostalgia has been a powerful force driving the Nova's popularity in recent years. As Baby Boomers and Generation X enter their peak earning years, many are seeking to recapture a piece of their youth. For countless Americans, the Nova represents the car they drove in high school, the one they wished they could afford, or the one that got away. This emotional connection translates directly into market demand, as collectors are often willing to pay premium prices for a slice of their own personal history.

The role of pop culture in maintaining the Nova's desirability cannot be overstated. Appearances in films, television shows, and music videos have kept the car in the public eye and introduced it to new generations of enthusiasts. Quentin Tarantino's "Death Proof," for example, featured a menacing black 1971 Nova, reigniting interest in the model among younger viewers. Such media exposure ensures that the Nova remains relevant and desirable, even as the car itself recedes further into history.

As we move further into the 21st century, the Chevy II Nova's status as a collector car icon seems secure. Its combination of historical significance, performance potential, and cultural cachet continues to attract enthusiasts from all walks of life. Whether viewed as a nostalgic touchstone, a savvy investment, or simply a beautiful piece of American automotive design, the Nova has firmly established itself as a star in the classic car firmament.

Section 11.2: Valuation and Investment Potential

The Chevy II Nova's ascent in the classic car market has transformed it from a humble family vehicle to a prized collector's item. Understanding the valuation and investment potential of classic cars is crucial for both seasoned collectors and newcomers to the classic car scene.

Current market values for different Nova models and years vary widely, reflecting the car's diverse production history. A well-maintained 1970 Nova SS, for instance, can command prices between $30,000 and $50,000, depending on specifications. Earlier models, particularly those from the first generation (1962-1965), typically fetch lower prices but are steadily appreciating as they become rarer. Late-model Novas from the mid-1970s, once overlooked, are now seeing increased interest, with prices for pristine examples starting to climb.

Several factors affect a Nova's value, with originality, documentation, and condition being paramount. Numbers-matching engines can significantly increase a Nova's value, sometimes by as much as 20% or more. Original paint, interiors, and components are highly prized, often commanding premium prices. Comprehensive documentation, including build sheets, original window stickers, and service records, can also boost a Nova's value by providing provenance and authenticity.

The impact of rarity on Nova values cannot be overstated. Limited editions and cars with rare factory options can fetch astronomical sums. The elusive 1970 Yenko Deuce Nova, with only a handful known to exist, can fetch over $500,000 at auction. Similarly, Novas equipped with rare engine options or unique color combinations often command significant premiums.

When considering the investment potential of a Nova, it's crucial to factor in restoration costs. A complete frame-off restoration can cost upwards of $50,000, but may increase the car's value by 100% or more. However, over-restoration can sometimes detract from a car's value, particularly if period-correct details are lost in the process. The key is to strike a balance between preservation and enhancement, maintaining the car's originality while ensuring its longevity and appeal.

Future projections for Nova values remain optimistic. Experts predict that rare, high-performance Novas will continue to appreciate by 5-10% annually over the next decade. This growth is driven by a combination of factors, including the car's cultural significance, the nostalgia of Baby Boomer and Gen X buyers, and the increasing rarity of well-preserved examples.

However, it's essential to note that not all Novas will be appreciated equally. Six-cylinder models and base trims, while still collectible, generally don't command the same premiums as V8-equipped cars or performance variants like the SS. That said, these more affordable models offer an excellent entry point for new collectors and can still provide enjoyment and modest appreciation.

The Nova's investment potential extends beyond mere financial returns. Many collectors find value in the joy of ownership, the camaraderie of the Nova community, and the satisfaction of preserving a piece of automotive history. This emotional component, while difficult to quantify, is an essential factor in the Nova's enduring appeal as a collector's item.

In conclusion, the Chevy II Nova presents a compelling case for investing in classic cars. With a wide range of models catering to various budgets, a passionate collector community, and a strong potential for appreciation, the Nova continues to shine in the classic car market. Whether you're drawn to the thrill of owning a piece of muscle car history or seeking a tangible investment with growth potential, the Nova offers a unique blend of nostalgia, performance, and financial opportunity.

Section 11.3: The Nova Collector Community

The Chevy II Nova has cultivated a passionate and dedicated community of collectors over the years, forming a tight-knit group bound by their shared love for this iconic American muscle car. This section delves into the heart of the Nova collector community, exploring the people, organizations, and events that keep the Nova spirit alive.

The typical Nova collector is a fascinating study in automotive enthusiasm. Most often, you'll find that the average Nova aficionado is a male in his 50s or 60s, with a deep-rooted passion for automotive history. These collectors usually have personal connections to the Nova, perhaps having owned one in their youth or admired it from afar during the car's heyday. Their motivations for collecting Novas are diverse, ranging from pure nostalgia to appreciation for the car's engineering, or even as a form of investment. Many Nova collectors are hands-on enthusiasts who enjoy the restoration process as much as the result, spending countless hours in their garages to bring these classic machines back to life.

Chevy II Nova: Power, Passion, and Performance

The Nova community has organized itself into various clubs and organizations dedicated to celebrating and preserving the legacy of the Chevy II Nova. One of the most prominent is the National Nostalgic Nova Network, boasting over 10,000 members across North America. These clubs serve multiple purposes: they act as social hubs for enthusiasts to share their passion, provide valuable resources for restoration and maintenance, and often advocate for the preservation of Novas as essential pieces of automotive history. Smaller, regional clubs also play a crucial role, organizing local meetups and providing a more intimate setting for Nova lovers to connect.

Major Nova-centric events and meetups form the backbone of the community's social calendar. The annual "Nova Nationals" stands out as the premier gathering, drawing thousands of Nova owners and spectators from across the country. This event typically features hundreds of pristine Novas on display, from bone-stock originals to wildly modified custom builds. Beyond the car show aspect, these events often include swap meets, technical seminars, and even drag racing events for those who like to push their Novas to the limit. These gatherings are not just about showing off cars; they're about forging friendships, sharing knowledge, and celebrating the enduring legacy of the Nova.

In the digital age, online communities and resources have become invaluable for Nova collectors. Websites like NovaResource.com have emerged as go-to platforms for enthusiasts seeking rare parts, expert advice, and connection with fellow collectors. These online forums allow Nova owners to troubleshoot problems, share restoration tips, and even track down those elusive, hard-to-find components that can make or break a restoration project. Social media groups dedicated to Novas have also flourished, providing instant connectivity and a constant stream of Nova-related content for enthusiasts to enjoy.

One of the most heartening aspects of the Nova collector community is the strong emphasis on mentorship. Recognizing the importance of passing down knowledge and skills to the next generation, many Nova clubs have established mentorship programs. These initiatives pair novice restorers with seasoned experts, ensuring that the art of Nova restoration is preserved and refined. This mentorship extends beyond just technical skills; experienced collectors often guide newcomers through the intricacies of the collector car market, helping them make informed decisions about purchases, restorations, and sales.

The Nova collector community is more than just a group of car enthusiasts; it's a thriving subculture that keeps the spirit of American muscle cars alive. Through their passion, dedication, and willingness to share knowledge, Nova collectors ensure that these beloved automobiles continue to captivate new generations of enthusiasts. As the community evolves, embracing both tradition and new technologies, it stands as a testament to the enduring appeal of the Chevy II Nova and its special place in automotive history.

Section 11.4: Challenges in Nova Collecting

Collecting and restoring Chevy II Novas can be a rewarding experience, but it's not without its challenges. As these classic cars become increasingly rare and sought after, enthusiasts face a unique set of challenges in their quest to own and maintain these iconic vehicles.

One of the most significant hurdles Nova collectors encounter is the scarcity of original parts. As time passes, finding authentic components for early Chevy II models becomes increasingly tricky. Trim pieces, interior elements, and specific mechanical parts can be tough to source, often requiring extensive searching or even custom fabrication. For instance, locating an original grille for a 1962 Chevy II might involve months of scouring swap meets, online marketplaces, and specialist dealers. This scarcity not only affects restoration projects but can also drive up the cost of maintaining these classics.

Authenticity verification is another critical challenge in Nova's collection process. With the rising values of these cars, the market has seen an increase in fraudulent claims and misrepresented vehicles. Collectors must become adept at VIN decoding, engine stamp analysis, and other authentication methods to ensure they're acquiring a genuine article. This process can be particularly complex for rare models or high-performance variants, where even minor details can significantly impact a car's value and desirability.

Storage and maintenance considerations present their own set of challenges for Nova collectors. These classic cars require specific care to preserve their condition and value. Proper climate-controlled storage is essential to prevent rust, deterioration of rubber components, and protect original interiors. Humidity control, for example, is crucial in preventing the formation of rust in hidden areas of the body. Additionally, regular maintenance routines must be adapted to suit the needs of older vehicles, which may require more frequent attention than modern cars.

Insurance and legal considerations add another layer of complexity to Nova's collection process. Standard auto insurance policies often fall short when it comes to protecting these valuable classics. Many collectors opt for agreed-value insurance policies to ensure full compensation in case of loss or damage. These specialized policies take into account the car's actual market value, including any restoration work or rare components. Navigating the legal landscape can also be tricky, especially when it comes to registering and driving vintage vehicles that may not meet modern safety or emissions standards.

One of the most philosophical challenges faced by Nova collectors is balancing preservation with drivability. The dilemma of whether to keep a car entirely original or to modify it for improved performance and safety is a constant debate in the collector community. Some purists insist on maintaining every aspect of their Nova in its original state, even if it means sacrificing some functionality. Others choose to make subtle upgrades, such as installing modern disc brakes or electronic ignition systems, to enhance safety and reliability without significantly altering the car's appearance or character.

This balance becomes particularly tricky when dealing with rare or historically significant Novas. For instance, a collector owning one of the few remaining original 1966 L79 Nova SS models might grapple with the decision to drive the car regularly, risking wear and tear, or to preserve it as a museum piece, potentially losing out on the joy of experiencing the vehicle on the road.

The restoration process itself presents numerous challenges. Deciding on the level of restoration ,whether to aim for a concours-quality showpiece or a driver-quality classic ,can have significant implications for both cost and the car's ultimate purpose. A full-frame-off restoration can efficiently run into tens of thousands of dollars and take years to complete. This level of investment necessitates careful consideration of the car's potential value after restoration and the owner's long-term objectives.

Furthermore, finding skilled artisans who understand the intricacies of classic car restoration is becoming increasingly complex. As older mechanics and body shop experts retire, their specialized knowledge of vintage vehicles, such as the Nova, becomes increasingly scarce. This shortage of expertise can lead to longer wait times for quality restoration work and higher costs for specialized services.

Despite these challenges, many Nova enthusiasts find that overcoming these obstacles is part of the appeal of collecting. Each hurdle surmounted adds to the sense of accomplishment and deepens their connection to their cherished vehicles. The process of sourcing rare parts, verifying authenticity, and maintaining these classics becomes a labor of love that goes beyond mere car ownership.

In the face of these challenges, the Nova collecting community has developed various resources and support networks. Online forums, specialty parts manufacturers, and restoration guides have emerged to help collectors navigate these complexities. Car clubs and Nova-specific organizations often serve as invaluable sources of knowledge, offering everything from technical advice to emotional support for fellow enthusiasts facing challenges in collecting.

As the classic car market continues to evolve, Nova collectors must stay informed and adaptable. The challenges of collecting these iconic vehicles are matched only by the passion of those who pursue them, ensuring that the Chevy II Nova will continue to hold a special place in automotive history for generations to come.

Section 11.5: Nova as an Investment Vehicle

The Chevy II Nova has transcended its original role as a practical family car to become a sought-after investment vehicle in the classic car market. This section examines the potential of Nova as a financial asset and offers insights for those considering adding these iconic cars to their investment portfolios.

When comparing Nova appreciation to traditional investments, the results are often surprising. While the S&P 500 has historically averaged around 10% annual returns, specific Nova models have appreciated by 15% or more per year. For instance, a well-maintained 1967 Nova SS that might have sold for $30,000 a decade ago could now command $75,000 or more in today's market. This impressive growth rate has caught the attention of investors looking to diversify beyond conventional financial instruments.

However, as with any investment, diversification within Nova collecting is key to managing risk and maximizing potential returns. A balanced Nova portfolio might include a mix of years, body styles, and performance levels. For example, an investor might combine a rare, high-performance 1970 Nova SS with a more common but well-preserved 1964 Chevy II sedan. This strategy enables collectors to capture value across various segments of the Nova market, potentially mitigating fluctuations in specific model valuations.

Understanding the tax implications of Nova's collection and sale is crucial for serious investors. Long-term capital gains taxes apply to Novas held for over a year, potentially reducing tax liability upon sale. For instance, if an investor purchased a Nova for $50,000 and sold it five years later for $80,000, they would only be taxed on the $30,000 profit, and at a lower rate than their ordinary income. However, it's essential to consult with a tax professional to navigate the complexities of classic car investments, especially for high-value transactions.

The role of auctions in the Nova market cannot be overstated. Major auction houses, such as Barrett-Jackson, Mecum, and RM Sotheby's, have played a significant role in establishing and promoting Nova values. These high-profile events often set benchmarks for the entire market. A prime example occurred when a rare 1967 Nova SS sold for a record-breaking $275,000 at Barrett-Jackson, setting a new standard for the model and elevating the perceived value of Novas across the board.

For those seeking to maximize returns on Nova investments, several proven practical strategies are available. Focusing on documented, numbers-matching examples often yields the best long-term investment results. These vehicles, with their original engines and verifiable histories, typically command premium prices and show stronger appreciation over time. Additionally, targeting limited production models or those with rare option combinations can lead to substantial returns. For example, a 1970 Nova with the seldom-seen L89 aluminum head option could be a far more lucrative investment than a standard SS model from the same year.

Restoration quality also plays a crucial role in investment potential. While over-restoration can sometimes detract from a car's value, a high-quality, period-correct restoration can significantly enhance a Nova's worth. Investors should seek out cars that have been restored to their original factory specifications using either original or correct reproduction parts.

Timing the market is challenging, but staying informed about trends in the classic car world can help investors make savvy decisions. Attending major car shows, following auction results, and engaging with the Nova community can provide valuable insights into market movements and emerging opportunities.

It's worth noting that while Novas can be excellent investments, they also offer something that stocks and bonds cannot: the joy of ownership and driving. Many Nova investors find that the intangible benefits of owning a piece of automotive history enhance the overall value of their investment.

In conclusion, the Chevy II Nova presents a unique investment opportunity in the classic car market. With strong appreciation potential, diverse options for portfolio building, and the added benefit of enjoyment, Novas offer a compelling case for inclusion in alternative investment strategies. However, as with any investment, due diligence, market knowledge, and a long-term perspective are essential for success in the world of Nova collecting.

Section 11.6: The Future of Nova Collecting

As we look ahead, the future of Nova collecting appears bright, with several trends and factors shaping its trajectory. The classic car market is continually evolving, and the Nova is well-positioned to remain a highly sought-after piece of automotive history.

One of the most significant trends is the increasing interest from younger generations. While Baby Boomers and Gen X have traditionally dominated the Nova collecting scene, Millennials are now entering the market with enthusiasm. This shift is partly driven by the popularity of resto-mod Novas, which combine classic aesthetics with modern performance and comfort. As a result, we're seeing a surge in demand for Novas that can be customized and upgraded, appealing to those who want a classic car experience without sacrificing modern amenities.

The rise of electric vehicle technology is also making its mark on Nova collecting. Some forward-thinking enthusiasts are exploring electric conversions for their classic Novas, preserving the iconic body style while embracing zero-emission powertrains. This trend could open up a whole new segment of the market, attracting environmentally conscious collectors who want to merge nostalgia with sustainability.

Digital technology is revolutionizing the way Nova enthusiasts connect and trade. Online marketplaces dedicated to classic cars are making it easier than ever to find and purchase Novas from around the world. Virtual reality and augmented reality technologies are also emerging as tools for collectors, allowing for detailed virtual inspections of vehicles before purchase. These innovations are likely to expand the global reach of Nova collecting, connecting buyers and sellers across continents.

The increasing rarity of original, unrestored Novas is another factor shaping the future of the collecting market. As time goes on, barn finds and survivor cars become increasingly scarce. This scarcity is driving up the value of original examples, particularly those with documented histories. In the coming years, we can expect to see a greater emphasis on provenance and originality, with collectors willing to pay premium prices for untouched Novas.

Climate change and environmental regulations may also impact Nova's collection in the future. As some cities consider restrictions on classic car usage to reduce emissions, collectors may need to adapt their practices. This could lead to increased interest in low-emission modifications or the creation of designated classic car zones in urban areas.

The future may also see the rise of fractional ownership in the Nova market. This model, already popular in other collectible markets, allows multiple investors to own shares of a high-value Nova. This could make rare, expensive models more accessible to a broader range of enthusiasts and potentially drive up values for the most desirable examples.

Lastly, as automotive technology continues to advance rapidly, the Nova's relative simplicity may become an even more attractive feature. In a world of increasingly complex, computer-controlled vehicles, the straightforward mechanics of a classic Nova offer a refreshing contrast. This could drive renewed interest in learning mechanical skills, with the Nova serving as an ideal platform for hands-on enthusiasts.

In conclusion, the future of Nova collecting is poised for growth and evolution. While challenges exist, the passion for these classic machines shows no signs of waning. Instead, new technologies, changing demographics, and shifting automotive landscapes are opening up exciting possibilities for Nova enthusiasts. As we move forward, the Chevy II Nova will undoubtedly continue to captivate collectors, serving as a tangible link to automotive history and a canvas for future innovations in the classic car world.

Section 11.7: The Future of Nova Collecting

As we look ahead, the future of Nova collecting appears bright and full of potential. The enduring appeal of this classic American muscle car shows no signs of waning, and several factors indicate that its popularity will continue to grow in the years to come.

One of the most significant trends shaping the future of Nova collecting is the increasing interest from younger generations. While Baby Boomers and Gen X have traditionally dominated the classic car market, Millennials and even some Gen Z enthusiasts are now entering the scene. These younger collectors are drawn to the Nova's blend of classic styling, performance potential, and relative affordability compared to some other muscle car icons. As they begin to accumulate disposable income and seek out nostalgic experiences, we can expect to see a surge in demand for well-preserved Novas.

Technological advancements are also playing a crucial role in shaping the future of Nova collecting. The rise of 3D printing and advanced manufacturing techniques is making it easier to reproduce rare or discontinued parts. This development is a double-edged sword for collectors. On one hand, it makes restoration projects more feasible and helps keep more Novas on the road. On the other hand, it may impact the value of original, numbers-matching vehicles. Savvy collectors will need to stay informed about these developments and adjust their strategies accordingly.

The growing emphasis on environmental consciousness is another factor that will influence Nova's collecting in the future. As regulations surrounding emissions and fuel efficiency become stricter, we may see an increase in the conversion of classic Novas to electric and hybrid vehicles. While purists might balk at the idea, these eco-friendly modifications could open up the world of Nova collecting to a new audience of environmentally conscious enthusiasts. It's not hard to imagine a future where a pristine, all-original Nova sits alongside its electric-converted counterpart in a collection.

Digital technology is also revolutionizing the way Nova enthusiasts connect and trade. Online marketplaces, virtual car shows, and augmented reality apps that allow collectors to visualize potential modifications are all becoming increasingly sophisticated. These digital tools are making it easier for Nova fans to find their dream cars, source parts, and share knowledge, regardless of their geographical location. As these platforms evolve, we can expect the

Nova collecting community to become even more global and interconnected.

The investment potential of Novas is likely to remain strong in the future, particularly for rare and well-documented examples. As the supply of original, unrestored Novas continues to dwindle, their value is expected to appreciate. However, the market may become more discerning, with a greater emphasis placed on provenance, documentation, and originality. Collectors who focus on acquiring the most desirable models with the best documentation will likely see the most significant returns on their investments.

Looking further ahead, the advent of autonomous vehicles and changing attitudes towards car ownership could actually boost the appeal of classics like the Nova. As everyday driving becomes increasingly automated, the visceral, hands-on experience of driving a classic Nova may become even more prized. The Nova could become a symbol of a bygone era of driving engagement, attracting collectors who crave a more connected driving experience.

Finally, the future of Nova collecting will likely see a continued blending of preservation and modernization. While there will always be a market for all-original examples, we can expect to see more resto-mod Novas that combine classic aesthetics with modern performance and comfort features. This trend could broaden the appeal of Novas to collectors who appreciate the classic look but desire contemporary driving dynamics.

In conclusion, the future of Nova collecting is poised for exciting developments. From shifting demographics and technological advancements to changing environmental considerations and evolving market dynamics, the world of Nova enthusiasm is poised to transform in intriguing ways. What remains constant, however, is the timeless appeal of this iconic American muscle car. As long as some appreciate automotive history, performance, and the sheer joy of

Chevy II Nova: Power, Passion, and Performance

driving, the Chevy II Nova will continue to hold a special place in the world of classic car collecting.

Chevy II Nova: Power, Passion, and Performance

Chapter 12: Legacy and Impact: The Chevy II Nova's Enduring Influence

Section 12.1: The Nova's Place in Automotive History

The Chevrolet Nova, born as the Chevy II, carved out a unique and enduring place in automotive history that extends far beyond its years of production. As a pioneering compact car design, the Nova represented a bold step for General Motors, challenging the notion that American cars needed to be large and unwieldy to be desirable. Its introduction in 1962 marked a significant shift in Chevrolet's approach to meeting changing consumer demands, setting a new standard for compact yet capable vehicles.

The Nova's influence on future Chevrolet models cannot be overstated. Its successful blend of compact size, versatile engine options, and attractive styling became a template for many subsequent Chevrolet offerings. The Nova's DNA can be traced through various Chevrolet lineages, from the later Camaro to the modern Cruze, showcasing how its design philosophy of efficiency without sacrificing performance continued to shape the brand's identity for decades.

Chevy II Nova: Power, Passion, and Performance

One of the Nova's most significant contributions to automotive history was its role in the evolution of the muscle car era. While initially conceived as a compact family car, the Nova's lightweight chassis proved to be the perfect platform for high-performance engines. The introduction of V8 options, particularly in the Super Sport (SS) models, helped bridge the gap between everyday drivers and high-performance enthusiasts. This versatility allowed the Nova to play a crucial part in democratizing performance, making speed and power accessible to a broader range of consumers and paving the way for the golden age of muscle cars.

Technologically, the Nova introduced several innovations that would become industry standards. Its unibody construction, while not entirely new, helped popularize this more rigid and lightweight design approach in the compact car segment. The Nova also served as a testbed for advancements in suspension technology, engine efficiency, and safety features that would later be incorporated into other GM vehicles.

The impact of the Nova extended beyond Chevrolet, influencing the designs and strategies of competitors across the automotive industry. As rival manufacturers scrambled to match the Nova's combination of compact size, performance potential, and affordability, the entire landscape of American car design began to shift. Competitors like Ford and Chrysler were compelled to reassess their compact offerings, ushering in a new era of innovation and competition that ultimately benefited consumers with a broader range of choices.

The Nova's legacy in automotive history is that of a catalyst. This vehicle arrived at the right time to challenge conventions, meet emerging needs, and inspire a generation of car designers and enthusiasts. Its ability to evolve from a humble compact to a performance icon while maintaining its core identity demonstrates why the Nova remains a significant chapter in the story of American automobiles. As we look back on the Nova's contributions, it's clear that this versatile Chevrolet did more than just fill a gap in the market; it helped shape the direction of automotive design and culture for years to come.

Section 12.2: Cultural Icon Status

The Chevy II Nova's influence extends far beyond its mechanical prowess, firmly cementing its place as a cultural icon that has left an indelible mark on American popular culture. This compact car's journey from dealership showrooms to the silver screen, airwaves, and literary pages is a testament to its enduring appeal and significance.

In the realm of film and television, the Nova has made numerous memorable appearances, often symbolizing youth, rebellion, or the quintessential American muscle car experience. From high-octane chase scenes to coming-of-age narratives, the Nova's presence on screen has helped solidify its status as a cultural touchstone. Notable appearances include the 1973 film "American Graffiti," where a 1962 Nova plays a pivotal role, and more recent features like "Death Proof" (2007), in which Kurt Russell's character drives a menacing black 1971 Nova.

The Nova's cultural impact resonates through the world of music as well. Numerous songs across various genres have name-dropped the Nova, using it as a metaphor for freedom, power, or nostalgia. From country ballads romanticizing cruising down back roads to rock anthems celebrating raw horsepower, the Nova has inspired musicians to capture the essence of American automotive culture in their lyrics.

In literature, the Nova has found its way into countless novels and memoirs, often serving as a character in its own right. Authors have used the Nova to evoke a sense of time and place, particularly when exploring themes of 1960s and 1970s Americana. The car's versatility in storytelling, from being a first car full of promise to a souped-up street racer, has made it a favorite among writers seeking to add authenticity to their narratives.

The Nova's representation in automotive advertising is another facet of its cultural icon status. Chevrolet's marketing campaigns featuring the Nova not only sold cars but also helped shape the American dream of the era. These advertisements, with their bold claims and eye-catching visuals, have become collectibles in their own right, offering a window into the aspirations and values of mid-20th-century America.

Perhaps most significantly, the Nova became a symbol of American youth culture during its heyday. It represented affordability and style for young buyers, while its performance variants appealed to the speed-hungry crowd. The Nova was more than just transportation; it was a statement of independence, a rite of passage, and for many, a first taste of the freedom that comes with owning a car.

The Nova's cultural impact has also spawned a wide array of artwork and memorabilia. From detailed scale models to vintage dealer promotional items, Nova-inspired creations continue to be sought after by collectors and enthusiasts. Contemporary artists have reimagined the Nova in paintings, sculptures, and digital art, keeping its aesthetic alive for new generations to appreciate.

This cultural icon status has ensured that the Chevy II Nova remains relevant long after its production ceased. It has transcended its role as a mere automobile to become a symbol of an era, a muse for creatives, and a cherished memory for those who lived through its golden age. The Nova's presence in popular culture serves as a bridge between generations, allowing younger enthusiasts to connect with the car's rich history and ensuring that its legacy continues to cruise through the American consciousness.

Section 12.3: Influence on the Chevrolet Brand

The Chevy II Nova's impact on the Chevrolet brand cannot be overstated. This versatile compact car played a crucial role in strengthening Chevrolet's market position during a time of intense competition and shifting consumer preferences. As American drivers began to seek out smaller, more efficient vehicles, the Nova provided Chevrolet with a compelling answer to this demand, allowing the brand to maintain its strong presence in the automotive marketplace.

The Nova's success contributed significantly to brand loyalty among Chevrolet customers. Many first-time car buyers who chose the Nova as their entry into the Chevrolet family often remained loyal to the brand throughout their lives, upgrading to larger or more luxurious Chevrolet models as their needs changed. This created a lasting customer base that helped sustain Chevrolet's success for decades to come.

Within Chevrolet's performance car lineup, the Nova carved out a unique niche. While it may not have been as flashy as the Camaro or as powerful as the Chevelle, the Nova SS models offered an accessible entry point into the world of muscle cars. This positioning allowed Chevrolet to capture a broader range of performance enthusiasts, from budget-conscious young drivers to those seeking a more understated power delivery.

The Nova's design language had a lasting impact on Chevrolet's overall aesthetic. Its clean lines, practical proportions, and subtle styling cues influenced the design of subsequent Chevrolet models across various segments. The Nova's ability to balance form and function served as a template for future Chevrolet vehicles, emphasizing the brand's commitment to creating cars that were both visually appealing and highly functional.

Perhaps most importantly, the Nova played a pivotal role in shaping Chevrolet's marketing strategies. The car's versatility allowed

Chevrolet to target a diverse range of consumers, from families seeking an economical daily driver to performance enthusiasts looking for a capable platform for modifications. This multi-faceted appeal taught Chevrolet valuable lessons in market segmentation and targeted advertising, strategies that would serve the brand well in the decades to follow.

The Nova's influence extended beyond its production years, inspiring Chevrolet to continue innovating in the compact car segment. The lessons learned from the Nova's success informed the development of future models, ensuring that Chevrolet remained competitive in an ever-evolving automotive landscape.

In essence, the Chevy II Nova became more than just a successful model for Chevrolet; it became a cornerstone of the brand's identity. Its ability to adapt to changing market conditions, appeal to a wide range of consumers, and consistently deliver on Chevrolet's promise of quality and performance helped solidify Chevrolet's position as a leading American automaker. The Nova's legacy continues to influence Chevrolet's approach to vehicle design, marketing, and brand positioning to this day, serving as a reminder of the enduring impact a well-conceived and executed vehicle can have on an entire automotive brand.

Section 12.4: Engineering Legacy

The Chevy II Nova's engineering legacy is a testament to its impact on automotive technology and design. Throughout its production run, the Nova introduced and refined numerous advancements that would shape the future of car manufacturing.

One of the most significant contributions of the Nova was in engine technology. The vehicle's versatile engine bay accommodated a wide range of powerplants, from economical inline-sixes to powerful V8s. This flexibility enabled Chevrolet to experiment with various engine configurations, resulting in innovations in fuel efficiency, power output, and reliability. The Nova's small-block V8 engines, in particular, became legendary for their performance and tunability, influencing engine design across the industry.

The Nova also made strides in chassis and suspension design. Its unitized body construction, which integrated the frame with the body for improved rigidity and weight reduction, was a forward-thinking approach that would become industry standard. The Nova's suspension systems, particularly in later models, struck a balance between comfort and performance that many competitors sought to emulate. The introduction of the F41 sport suspension package in 1968 demonstrated how a compact car could deliver handling comparable to larger, more expensive vehicles.

In terms of safety, the Nova played a crucial role in advancing automotive safety features. As safety regulations became more stringent in the late 1960s and early 1970s, the Nova served as a platform for implementing and refining new safety technologies. These included improved brake systems, collapsible steering columns, and reinforced body structures designed better to protect occupants in the event of a collision. The Nova's evolution in safety features reflected the changing priorities of the automotive industry and contributed to raising safety standards across all vehicle categories.

The Nova's influence extended beyond its own production line, significantly impacting future GM platforms. The X-body platform, which underpinned the Nova, proved to be a versatile foundation that GM would adapt for various models across its brands. This platform-sharing approach, refined through the Nova's development, allowed GM to streamline production processes and reduce costs while offering a diverse range of vehicles to consumers. The lessons learned from the Nova's platform would inform the development of subsequent GM architectures, influencing vehicle design well into the future.

One of the most enduring aspects of the Nova's engineering legacy is its impact on performance tuning and modification. The Nova's combination of a lightweight body and potent engine options made it a favorite among hot rodders and performance enthusiasts. This popularity drove the development of a vast aftermarket industry dedicated to enhancing the Nova's performance capabilities. From high-performance camshafts to custom suspension kits, the innovations born from modifying Novas would have a profound influence on the broader world of automotive performance upgrades.

The engineering principles embodied in the Nova adaptability, efficiency, and performance continue to resonate in modern automotive design. Its legacy serves as a reminder of the innovative spirit that drove American car manufacturing during a transformative era. Today, as the automotive industry faces new challenges and opportunities, the lessons learned from the Nova's development and evolution continue to inform engineering decisions, ensuring that its influence extends far beyond its years in production.

Section 12.5: Collector Car Market Impact

The Chevy II Nova's impact on the collector car market is a testament to its enduring appeal and historical significance. As the years have passed, the Nova has solidified its position as a highly sought-after classic, with specific models and years commanding impressive prices at auctions and in private sales.

In the pantheon of classic American automobiles, the Nova occupies a unique space. While it may not command the astronomical prices of some rare muscle cars, it has consistently maintained a strong presence in the collector market. This is due in part to its versatility – from the early compact models to the later high-performance variants, there's a Nova to suit nearly every taste and budget.

Chevy II Nova: Power, Passion, and Performance

Several factors drive the collectibility of the Nova. First and foremost is nostalgia. For many baby boomers and Gen Xers, the Nova represents their youth, whether it was their first car, the car they dreamed of owning, or simply a ubiquitous presence on the streets of their childhood. This emotional connection translates directly into market demand.

Another key factor is the Nova's role in the muscle car era. While not always considered an actual muscle car, high-performance models like the Nova SS have become increasingly valuable. These cars offer a combination of power and style that resonates with collectors who appreciate the golden age of American performance automobiles.

The Nova's relatively simple mechanicals and abundant availability of replacement parts also contribute to its appeal among collectors. Unlike some rare classics that can be challenging and expensive to restore, many Nova models are comparatively easy to bring back to their former glory. This accessibility has helped maintain a robust market for these cars.

When examining price trends, it's clear that the Nova has shown steady appreciation over the years. While not as volatile as some high-end collector cars, Novas have provided solid returns for those who invested wisely. Of course, as with any collector car, condition is paramount. Well-preserved or expertly restored examples command the highest prices, with original documentation and matching numbers further boosting value.

Among Nova enthusiasts, specific models and years are considered the most desirable. The 1966-1967 Chevy II Nova SS models, particularly those equipped with the L79 327-cubic-inch V8, are highly prized. The 1968-1972 Nova SS models, especially those with big-block engines, are also top performers in the collector market. For fans of early Novas, the 1962-1965 Chevy II 400 models in excellent condition have seen increasing interest and value.

It's worth noting that the Nova's popularity in the collector market has had a ripple effect on related GM models. Cars that shared platforms or components with the Nova, such as the Pontiac Ventura or Oldsmobile Omega, have seen increased interest from collectors looking for alternatives to the more common Nova. This phenomenon demonstrates that the Nova's influence extends beyond its own marque, impacting the broader GM classic car ecosystem.

As we look to the future, all indicators suggest that the Nova will remain a strong performer in the collector car market. Its combination of historical significance, performance potential, and accessibility ensures its ongoing appeal to both seasoned collectors and newcomers to the classic car hobby. Whether as a cherished piece of automotive history or as an investment vehicle, the Chevy II Nova has carved out a lasting place in the collector car landscape, cementing its legacy for generations to come.

Section 12.6: Restoration and Preservation Movement

The Chevy II Nova's enduring popularity has given rise to a vibrant restoration and preservation movement, ensuring that these classic vehicles continue to captivate enthusiasts for generations to come. This movement has not only kept Novas on the road but has also spawned a thriving ecosystem of resources, businesses, and communities dedicated to preserving the Nova legacy.

One of the most significant developments in the Nova restoration world has been the growth of resources specific to Nova restoration. As the demand for authentic parts and accurate information has increased, numerous books, online forums, and video tutorials have emerged, catering specifically to Nova enthusiasts. These resources cover everything from basic maintenance to complete frame-off restorations, empowering owners to tackle projects of any scale. Detailed factory manuals have been reprinted, and new step-by-step guides have been created, ensuring that even novice restorers can approach their projects with confidence.

Chevy II Nova: Power, Passion, and Performance

The Nova's popularity has also had a profound influence on the aftermarket parts industry. Recognizing the strong demand from restorers, manufacturers have stepped up to produce a wide array of reproduction parts. From body panels and interior trim to engine components and suspension pieces, virtually every part of a Nova can now be sourced new. The availability of high-quality reproduction parts has enabled the restoration of even severely deteriorated Novas to their former glory. Additionally, performance upgrade parts explicitly designed for Novas have proliferated, allowing owners to enhance their cars while maintaining a period-correct appearance.

Nova restoration has evolved from a niche hobby into a full-fledged profession for many. Specialized restoration shops focusing exclusively on Novas and other GM compacts have sprung up across the country. These experts have developed techniques and processes specific to Nova restoration, ensuring that each project is completed to the highest standards. The restoration community has also fostered a new generation of artisans skilled in the art of metal shaping, upholstery work, and mechanical rebuilding, all tailored to the unique needs of Nova restoration.

Preservation efforts extend beyond individual restorations, with museums and collectors playing a crucial role in safeguarding the Nova's history. Automotive museums across the country now feature Novas in their exhibits, often showcasing rare or historically significant models. Private collectors have also taken up the mantle of preservation, assembling impressive collections of original and restored Novas. These preserved examples serve as valuable references for restorers and as time capsules of automotive history for future generations.

The passion for Nova restoration and preservation is most evident in the numerous Nova-centric car shows and events that take place annually. From small local gatherings to large national conventions, these events bring together Nova enthusiasts from diverse backgrounds. They provide a platform for owners to showcase their restorations, share knowledge, and celebrate the Nova's legacy. These events often feature judged competitions, which have helped establish and maintain high standards for Nova restorations.

The restoration and preservation movement surrounding the Chevy II Nova is a testament to the car's enduring appeal and historical significance. It has not only kept these classic vehicles on the road but has also created a community united by a shared passion for them. Through the efforts of dedicated enthusiasts, skilled craftsmen, and forward-thinking businesses, the Nova continues to thrive long after its production ceased. This movement ensures that future generations will have the opportunity to experience the unique charm and performance of the Chevy II Nova, preserving an important chapter in American automotive history.

Section 12.7: The Nova's Enduring Appeal

The Chevrolet Nova's enduring appeal is a testament to its timeless design, versatile performance, and the deep emotional connections it has forged with generations of automotive enthusiasts. This section explores the various factors that contribute to the Nova's enduring popularity and its ability to captivate new audiences decades after its production ceased.

One of the primary drivers of the Nova's enduring appeal is the strong nostalgia factor it holds for baby boomers and Generation X. For many in these age groups, the Nova represents more than just a car; it's a tangible link to their youth, a reminder of first dates, summer road trips, and the freedom of the open road. This emotional connection has kept the Nova relevant and desirable long after it ceased production, with many original owners and admirers seeking to recapture a piece of their past through ownership or restoration projects.

Chevy II Nova: Power, Passion, and Performance

However, the Nova's appeal isn't limited to those who experienced it firsthand during its heyday. Remarkably, the car continues to attract new generations of enthusiasts who appreciate its classic lines, straightforward mechanics, and the stories it represents. Younger car lovers are drawn to the Nova's simplicity and analog nature, viewing it as a refreshing alternative to modern, tech-laden vehicles. This cross-generational appeal has helped maintain the Nova's popularity and ensure its place in automotive culture for years to come.

The Nova has also found a significant role in the growing "restomod" movement, which combines classic car aesthetics with modern performance and comfort upgrades. This trend has breathed new life into many Novas, allowing owners to enjoy the car's iconic looks while benefiting from contemporary engineering advancements. Restomod Novas often feature updated engines, improved suspension systems, and modern amenities like air conditioning and advanced sound systems, making them more practical for everyday use while preserving their classic charm.

In the digital age, the Nova's appeal has expanded beyond physical gatherings to online communities and social media platforms. Enthusiast forums, Facebook groups, and Instagram accounts dedicated to the Nova have created virtual spaces where owners and admirers can share restoration tips, showcase their cars, and connect with like-minded individuals from around the world. These online communities have played a crucial role in sustaining interest in the Nova, providing a wealth of information and support for those looking to purchase, restore, or simply appreciate these classic vehicles.

Looking to the future, the Nova's enduring appeal suggests potential for future revivals or tributes. While Chevrolet has not announced any plans to resurrect the Nova nameplate, the automotive industry's current trend of reviving classic models leaves the door open for the possibility. Whether through a modern reinterpretation of the Nova or limited-edition tribute models, the car's lasting popularity could make it a candidate for future projects that blend nostalgia with contemporary design and technology.

The Nova's ability to remain relevant and desirable decades after its last production year is a remarkable achievement. It speaks to the car's initial design strengths, its cultural significance, and the passionate community that has grown around it. As automotive trends come and go, the Nova stands as a beacon of classic American car culture, continuing to inspire, excite, and connect enthusiasts across generations. Its enduring appeal ensures that the Chevy II Nova will remain a cherished icon in the automotive world for many years to come, bridging the past, present, and future of car enthusiasm.

ABOUT THE AUTHOR

Todd Bandel is an accomplished author specializing in informational history books, with a particular focus on the automotive industry. Drawing from 40 years of experience as an automotive technician, Todd combines deep expertise and passion to enlighten readers about the historical nuances of automobiles. Todd currently resides in San Diego, California, where he continues to explore and write about his enduring interest in automotive history.

Mechanicaddicts.com

www.ingramcontent.com/pod-product-compliance
Lightning Source LLC
LaVergne TN
LVHW051233080426
835513LV00016B/1560